The Big Book of

TERRIFIC

TEACHING IDEAS

For Jewish Supplementary Schools,
Day Schools, Youth Groups,
Camps, and Retreats

SHIRLEY BARISH

Illustrated by

ANN D. KOFFSKY

URJ Press   •   New York, New York

Naomi
We are very
grateful to
you for your help
+ guidance in the
Jewish education
Center. Wishing
you continued success
in your personal
journey in Jewish
Education.
Fondly,
Ellyn Kaufman
26 Tevet 5775
Jan 17, 2015

Library of Congress Cataloging-in-Publication Data

Barish, Shirley.
    The big book of terrific teaching ideas / Shirley Barish ; illustrated by Ann D. Koffsky.
        p. cm.
    ISBN 0-8074-0806-9 (pbk. : alk. paper)
    1. Judaism--Study and teaching. 2. Judaism--Study and teaching--Activity programs. 3. Jewish religious education of children. 4. Jewish religious education of teenagers. I. Title: Terrific teaching ideas. II. Title.

BM103.B365 2004
296.6'8--dc22

                                                              2004041296

This book is dedicated to the woman who opened her heart and arms to my family. She truly became our mother. During her ninety-seven years she *kvelled* with pride over my achievements, and adored her grandchildren and great-grandchildren. She was the queen, the matriarch, of our family. On September 1, 2000, she left us; though we mourned her passing, we celebrated her grand life. Therefore this book is dedicated in heartfelt thanks to the memory of Eleanor Fenberg for all she was for me and my family.

Shirley Barish

Contents

Junior and Senior High School

Helpful Hints

Kindergarten–Primary Grades

This is probably my favorite age group. Young children are still eager and willing to learn. They do not have all the distractions that are common to the older students. The synagogue is still a safe haven for these youngsters, and the teacher is the center of their focus while they are in class.

You will find a wide variety of activities in this chapter, covering holidays, Bible, Jewish values, and more. These activities can easily be adapted to any of the ages in this group of children. The secret with young children is to keep them moving—their attention span is not very long. Even given their eagerness to learn, they still like variety, just as older students do. Using a variety of approaches, a different one each week, keeps children coming back for more.

Jewish Holidays

SHABBAT

From Beginning to End

This idea comes from the Bureau of Jewish Education in Houston. Prepare index cards that show all the different parts of the Shabbat celebration, beginning with *Erev Shabbat* on Friday and ending with *Havdalah* on Saturday evening. Use pictures from old workbooks or draw the pictures you need. On each index card, place a picture and the appropriate prayer (if it applies) that goes with the picture. Include Hebrew, transliteration, and English. Your Shabbat cards could include the following (note that you are not limited to this list):

Erev Shabbat
Preparation for Shabbat
Making challah
Cooking Shabbat dinner
Family at dinner table
Shabbat candle lighting
Kiddush
HaMotzi
Eating dinner
Birkat HaMazon
Singing *z'mirot* after dinner

Yom Shabbat
Eating breakfast
Getting ready to go to synagogue
Synagogue worship
Torah study
Kiddush luncheon
Shabbat rest
S'udah Sh'lishit
Havdalah

Laminate the completed cards or cover them with clear contact paper.

Shuffle the cards, then have the children place them in the correct order. If you make multiple sets of cards, the children can work in teams to see who completes the task first. Or, the children could create a Shabbat time line across one wall of your classroom.

Welcoming Shabbat

Give the children art or construction paper and crayons or markers. Have children draw pictures of how they would welcome Shabbat into their home.

2

Let's Celebrate Shabbat

Children love opening presents. Make it even more fun by wearing a special outfit or apron with *large* patch pockets. Into these pockets, place "surprises" that have to do with Shabbat. Your objective for the day is for the children to learn the different symbols and blessings of Shabbat. You will need a small pair of candlesticks, a wooden challah, a miniature challah cover, a small wooden bottle of wine, and a wooden kiddush cup. All of the above items can be found in most Judaic stores or catalogs. To really get the children's attention have miniature bottles of grape juice and challah for each child. It is more fun to learn the symbols and blessings with the real thing, and they get to eat and drink it, too.

Wrap each item as a present—remember children love to open presents—and place them in your pockets. When all the children are settled, announce to them that today we are going to have a celebration and that with all celebrations we open presents. All the children are going to want to open a present so try to have a little something for each one, even if you need to duplicate items. Use a tote bag if you don't have enough pockets. One at a time, let a child reach into one of your pockets and pick out a "present." Let the child open it and describe what he or she finds. You then tell what, when, and how the item is used during Shabbat. Introduce the blessing for the symbol and have the children repeat it after you word for word. Then go on to the next present. Continue until all the items are unwrapped and children have said the blessing at least once for each symbol.

Once all the presents are open, have one student choose a symbol and help that child repeat the blessing. Give more children turns to repeat the blessings for the different symbols of Shabbat. The young children are going to learn from repetition. To involve the parents, make up sheets containing a picture of each symbol, with the blessing next to the picture in Hebrew, transliteration, and English. Send it home with the children to practice at home with their parents and siblings. As closure, give the children a chance to practice with the real thing. Have grape juice and challah handy; let kids say the appropriate blessings and then have a snack!

TU BISH'VAT

Plant Your Trees and Eat Them, Too

This is a celebration for the New Year of the trees. You can still plant trees, but with this activity you can give the children a treat at the same time. For each child, you will need the following:

a "flower pot"—a paper or styrofoam cup

"mud"—instant chocolate pudding mix and milk

"dirt"—crushed chocolate cookies (Use a blender or food processor to crush.)

a "tree trunk"—a plastic spoon will do nicely (You can find brown spoons at party good stores.)

a paper treetop and tape

Directions

1. Give each child a "flower pot."
2. Have students put the "mud" in the pot, then sprinkle with "dirt."
3. Tape the treetop to the "trunk." Younger children may need help. The tree top should be taped to the handle of the spoon.
4. Plant the "tree" in the "mud" and "dirt." Ooh and aah over the creations, and let the children eat the treats with the "tree trunks."

PURIM

Picture the Story

Gather together pictures that tell the story of Purim. Show them to the children as you tell the story, talking with the children about what the pictures show. After the story is told, mix up the pictures and let the children place them in the correct order.

PESACH

Nut Cups for Pesach

The kids have fun with this, so you might need more than one per child.

You will need:
clear plastic 3 oz. or 5 oz. cups

colored tissue paper

ribbon

white glue

paintbrushes

Directions:

1. Cut tissue paper into one-inch squares and dilute some white glue with water.
2. Paint a coat of diluted glue on the outside of the cup.
3. Place tissue paper in a mosaic effect around the cup until the whole cup is covered.
4. Using undiluted glue, glue a length of ribbon around the open edge of the cup.
5. Allow all to dry. Students take them home to use as nut cups for the Seder table.

ACTIVITIES FOR ANY JEWISH HOLIDAY

Hide Some Pictures

You can make your own hidden picture for any Jewish holiday. Gather together copies of small pictures of Jewish symbols and ritual objects for your choice of holiday. Next, find a picture that is pleasing to the eye, or make your own with trees, hills, flowers, lakes, and so forth. Paste the symbol pictures all around the picture, "hiding" them throughout the picture. Make copies for the children. Students are to find the hidden pictures and draw a circle around each one. When children have finished, talk about the hidden items and their relationship to the holiday.

Matching Holiday Foods

A number of our Jewish holidays have special foods related to them. You can prepare a sheet with a list of the holidays that could look something like this:

Rosh HaShanah: apples and honey; round challah

Tu BiSh'vat: fruits and nuts

Chanukah: potato latkes and doughnuts

Purim: hamantashen

Pesach: matzah; parsley; *charoset,* gefilte fish, matzah ball soup

Shavuot: cheese blintzes

Shabbat: challah; wine

Write the list of the holidays on the left side of a sheet of paper. Draw blank boxes or plates for the food on the right side, opposite the holidays.

Gather together pictures sized to fit in the space provided. Paste these pictures on another sheet of paper. Copy both sheets for the students and distribute them.

Have children cut out the food items and place them in their appropriate space on the holiday sheet. After they have completed the activity, talk about the different foods and their relationship to the holiday.

What We Can Learn from Our Elders

Encourage the students to question their grandparents or the elderly members of the congregation to find out how they celebrated the holiday you are studying when they were children. With the students, develop a questionnaire they can use for their interviews. The questionnaire could include the following:

When and where did the celebration take place?
How long did you celebrate the holiday?
Who came to the celebration?
What did you eat? Were any special foods served?
What did you do? Did you play any games related to the holiday?
What kind of clothes did you wear?

Give the students a few weeks to gather their information, then ask them to prepare a report. The report can be a combination of words and drawings, along with any pictures students might have obtained. After all the reports are given, compare the similarities and differences among the celebrations.

Fill in a Picture

Create and copy a simple picture so the children can fill in missing details from the instructions you will provide. For example, for a lesson on Pesach, have a picture of an empty table with some chairs around it. You then might give instructions such as the following:

1. Draw a seder plate on the table.
2. Draw the items that go on the seder plate.
3. Draw a pillow on each chair.
4. Draw a plate with matzah.

5. Draw a place setting for each chair.
6. Draw a Haggadah next to each setting.
7. Draw Elijah's cup (and Miriam's cup).

Go over the items and see if the children know what each one is and how it is used during the holiday. Add your own explanations as needed.

A Holiday Table Drawing

Have children divide an 8½ x 11 sheet of paper into three columns headed "On the Table," "Under the Table," and "Next to the Table." (The "Under the Table" column is for the fun of it, to allow the kids to be creative.) Divide the class into small groups. Have children list what is placed on, under, and next to the table for a specific Jewish holiday. Each group must be ready to defend its choices. Children then draw the table, including all the items they have listed. Share the finished drawings with the class.

Push the Button

Have each student draw a picture that represents some part of your unit of study. For example, for a unit on Shabbat, assign each child a different symbol, food, ritual, or other element of the Shabbat celebration. Each student is to use what he or she learned about the class subject, then draw a picture (or pictures) representing that assignment. The outline of a button should be drawn in a corner of each picture. Explain to the children that when their parents visit (or when you send home the drawing), the parent is to push the button. When the button is pushed, the student stands up and tells all about his or her picture and what it means. This gives children an opportunity to show what they have learned.

Charades

Over the years I have heard the children say that all they study in religious school are the holidays. This activity draws on knowledge they already have and can be a fun way to review the different holidays.

Make a list of different activities that can be performed during a specific Jewish holiday. Place each activity on an index card. Shuffle the cards well and place them facedown on the desk. Have a student select a card and perform the charade activity. Allow the class to identify the action. Continue until everyone has had a turn.

Alternative

If you really want to have some fun, try one of these approaches. Write each activity on a slip of paper and place it in a balloon. Blow up the balloons and hang them around the room. Each child selects a balloon, pops it, and acts out the activity. Or, write the activity on a sheet of paper and then make a paper airplane. Fly each airplane at a child, who then performs a charade of the activity.

Young People Tell a Story

Show a picture of a Jewish symbol, of a family having a Shabbat dinner or Pesach seder, or of any other holiday activity. Invite a child in the class to come up and tell a story about what he or she sees in the picture. As the child tells the story, write it on chart paper (or have an aide do so) for everyone to see. When the child finishes the story, cut it into sentence strips. Give each child a sentence, as well as some drawing paper and crayons, and ask students to draw a picture that goes with their sentence. Then have students work together to present their illustrated sentences into story order. Compile into a finished storybook and display it on the wall or on the table.

Holiday Tablecloth

This activity works well for those holidays with specific table rituals and foods. Take a large piece of art or butcher paper. It needs to be big enough for the children to sit around it on the floor. Have available crayons or markers for the children to use. Talk about the holiday and its special rituals and goods. Have each child, sitting at his or her "tablecloth space," draw a picture of a table setting with all the ritual objects and foods necessary for the holiday. After the children have completed the tablecloth, have a holiday party using the tablecloth they designed.

The Right Word or Picture

Gather together pictures of the rituals, symbols, and activities of a number of Jewish holidays. This activity can be done individually or as a whole class. If you do it individually make at least two pages' worth of pictures; have copies for each student. If you do this as a class activity, enlarge the pictures and place them on the bulletin board, make a big poster of them, or just attach them to the blackboard.

Prepare a list of tasks for the children to do. For example, have them circle (or point to) the picture that

- doesn't belong with (name the holiday).
- is the food we eat on (name the holiday).
- shows what we do on (name the holiday).

Picture Story

Young children may not be able to read, but they can certainly match pictures to words *you* read. Based on your unit of study, gather together pictures that represent the holiday, including symbols and special foods. Mount the pictures on card stock; laminate or cover with clear contact paper. Then prepare sentence strips that when combined will create a story. Your story line could look something like this:

Mother/Father cooks for Shabbat.
Children set the table.
Candlesticks are placed on the table.
A *Kiddush* cup is placed on the table.
A covered challah is placed on the table.
The family sits at the table.
Candles are lit.
The children are blessed.
Kiddush is said.
The challah is uncovered and blessed.
The family eats dinner.

Mix up and display the pictures around the room. Show the children the first sentence and read it. Ask them to choose the picture that goes with the sentence. Have a child place the picture with the sentence. Continue until the "picture story" has been placed in the proper sequence.

Holiday Dress Up

Get some large brown grocery store paper bags. Cut a vest out of each bag, one per child. You will also need some cutouts of holiday symbols—use brightly colored paper—plus glue, markers, and other decorating items.

As you study the holiday, be sure the children learn all the different aspects: when it is celebrated, how we celebrate it, and why we are celebrating. Tell them we dress up for the holidays. Give out the paper vests, telling children they are to be decorated especially for this holiday. Give students some time to talk about how they will decorate their vests, then let them loose.

Make up a Story

Take one of the symbols or ritual objects for the holiday you are reviewing. Write or find a short story about that object or symbol. Share it with the children. Then break into small groups and have each group write its own short story or poem about the object. Have each group share its creation. Tape record their efforts or place all the writings together in a booklet. Each child can design a cover for his or her own book and take the book home to share with family members.

Holiday Acrostic

Students place the name of their favorite Jewish holiday down the left side of a sheet of paper in capital letters. Next to each letter they are to write a word or two that tells something about the holiday. Do this with each letter. Here is an example:

Study of Torah
Holy day
After-dinner singing
Baking challah
Being with family
After-worship *oneg*
Time to rest

Allow students to share their completed acrostic.

Crack the Clues

This activity can be used for any holiday. Using 4 x 6 index cards, write on each one the name of a different symbol or ritual object. Have one index card for each student. Pass out the cards, telling the students to keep the item a secret; they are not to tell any of their classmates. Have students write three clues to help the class identify the item. For example, if the item is "Shabbat candles," the three clues could be as follows:

- There are usually two of them.
- They signal the start of the holiday.
- They burn many different colors.

10

Give students an opportunity to present their clues, one at a time. After each clue is presented, the class sees if it can identify the object. The person who identifies the word then has a turn. If a child has already gone, he or she gets to choose who goes next.

Time to Enjoy the Holidays

Ask the students what their favorite Jewish holiday is. What makes it their favorite? What do they do to celebrate, and how is the family involved? What makes this Jewish celebration so unique for them? Give children time to really talk about their favorite holidays.

After the discussion is finished, give each student an 8½ x 11 piece of white drawing paper and some scratch paper. Ask students to draw a picture of something special they do on their favorite Jewish holiday. Have them use the scratch paper to outline the picture they want to draw. When they are satisfied with the design, they can do their art work on the drawing paper, leaving room at the top or bottom to write a short descriptive sentence for the picture. Give students time to complete their art work. Have students use a "frame" of 9 x 12 construction paper. Have students glue the frames to the pictures. If time permits, allow students to decorate the frames. After each child has described the event taking place in his or her picture, display the pictures on the bulletin board or around the room.

Mix-and-Match Puzzles

This is a variation of an old theme. Cut out a variety of Jewish symbols and ritual objects from the same color card stock. After you have cut out the objects, cut off a portion of each one. Keep in mind that the very young may have difficulty manipulating small pieces. Mix well and spread all the parts of your "puzzle" on the table. The students are to match the pieces correctly and then name the object, if possible explaining when and where it is used. If students do not know, the activity becomes a good introduction to the day's lesson.

Jewish Values, Concepts, and Symbols

L'SHON HARA

Although dealing with *l'shon hara* is discussed in the "Helpful Hints" section of this book (see pages 165–166), you may wish to do a whole unit on the subject.

Dramatic Skits

Divide your class into small groups of three to four students. Give each group a one-line description of an insult that someone might say, for example:

That new girl is stupid.
That boy is a nerd because he doesn't like to play football.
I don't want her on my team because she runs too slowly.

Each group is to create a short three-minute skit based on the statement. The skit should reveal how that person must feel and what the group could do about the situation. Give the groups time to rehearse before performing the skits. After each presentation, allow students to make additional comments about how they might have handled the situation.

Hurtful Words

There is a midrash about a woman whom a rabbi tells to pluck a chicken and let the feathers blow in the wind when she wants to be forgiven for her "hurtful" words and gossip. When he tells her to gather them all up, she says that it is impossible. This midrash appears in a children's picture book by Joan Rothenberg called *Yettele's Feathers* and as a story in Molly Cone's *Who Knows Ten?* Feel free to use these to present the story to the class. You can buy a bag of feathers from a craft store and reenact the story with your students or you can use a tube of toothpaste and a paper plate.

Ask one of the students to squeeze all the toothpaste out on the paper plate. Compare how easy that is to gossiping and saying hurtful words to classmates and others. Then ask for another volunteer. This one is to gather up all the toothpaste and put it back where it came from. Naturally, students soon find that it can't be done. Remind them that so it is with hurtful words and gossip: They can't be taken back or forgotten.

What Would You Do If . . .

Our Jewish tradition tells us to help others, feed the hungry, leave the corners of the field for the poor to harvest, take care of the widow and orphan, and so on. We learn that treating people with respect is an essential Jewish value. How many of us believe in these words, and if we do, when do we take the time to transmit them to our children?

We often overlook opportunities to ask kids "What would you do if . . . ?" These kind of conversations are really rehearsals that can enable children to make choices. Sometimes the choices they make aren't those you would like to see them make. Still, by simply sharing with children how you make a choice or how you would handle difficult moral dilemmas, you are not "telling" them they are wrong; rather, you are presenting them with a more positive role model. These conversations are inherently Jewish and students will learn from them—maybe not right at the moment, but when faced with a problem, they will remember.

So take some time, as part of a lesson, to ask, "What would you do if . . . ?" Here are a few examples to get you started, then you think up your own:

What would you do if . . .

- You see some big kids picking on another kid?
    a. Join in, or they might pick on you.
    b. Just stand there and do nothing.
    c. Tell them to stop; or, if that's too scary, get a grown-up to stop them.

- Your best friend wants to tell you a secret?
    a. Promise not to tell, but then you blurt it out anyway as soon as you see another friend.
    b. Tell your friend that secrets are stupid.
    c. Promise not to say a word to anyone—and then don't.

- Your best friend, whom you haven't seen all summer, comes back to school with the worst haircut you have ever seen and she asks you what you honestly think of it?
    a. Say: "That's the worst haircut ever!"
    b. Say: "Now that's what I call a haircut."
    c. Say: "I think the cut you had last spring was better."

- Some of your friends are always gossiping about another friend of yours?
    a. Join in with some really juicy gossip.
    b. Stay quiet because you are trying to stay friends with everyone.
    c. Consider changing friends because these are too mean!

- Somebody gives the wrong answer to an easy question in class?
    a. Shout out the right answer so everyone knows how smart you are.
    b. Laugh yourself silly.
    c. Say nothing—next time it might be you!

Words into Deeds

Prepare a cutout silhouette of a person and have prepared cutout magazine pictures or drawings of ways people can help others. Guide the children to name a person who often helps other people. Talk with them about how this person helps others. Let the children select the pictures that fit the person they chose. Glue the pictures onto the silhouette and hang it up. Next, give children drawing paper and crayons, telling them to draw pictures of how they themselves can help other people. Display students' work around the silhouette.

Invite children to go over their drawings, letting the children tell the different ways they can help people. Help the children choose one activity (or more) they would like to do as a "helping others" project. Once the decision is made, help them make plans to follow through on the project.

Building a House of *G'milut Chasadim*

Instead of a tree, build a house! Once the students have a good idea of what *g'milut chasadim* is, tell them they can help build a "House of *G'milut Chasadim*" with each deed they perform. Have prepared some *g'milut chasadim* slips, four or five to a page. Each strip should have a place for the student's name and a line stating: "Deed performed: _____," with space for the student to complete what he or she did and for whom. Each week, when a student turns in a sheet, give the student a block or Lego to add to the "construction of the house." If you have a small class, give students each two or three so they can see some progress. If the whole school participates—which would be a great idea—give one block or Lego for each deed performed. So the whole school can see, place the "house" in a prominent place; the entire congregation can watch it grow. Before you know it, your House of *G'milut Chasadim* will be taking shape and a bunch of kids will be putting their Jewish values to work.

Tzedakah Box

Some of you may remember those little blue boxes your parents or grandparents had on the mantel or shelf. Perhaps, before Shabbat began, you cleaned out your pockets of change and placed it in the box. In my home, money from the blue box, or *pushke,* went to the Jewish National Fund. Every Friday night, before dinner, we put our change in the *tzedakah* box before the Shabbat candles were lit. Not many of our children know about this tradition and it would be nice to re-create it, beginning with the younger children.

Briefly, talk to the children about giving, sharing the different ways we give *tzedakah*. If possible, give an example of your own experience with the *tzedakah* box (or use my experience). Ask the children how they could get their families to participate in the giving of *tzedakah*. Really talk it through, helping children as needed. Have them make *tzedakah* boxes and take them home, along with a list of all their ideas. There are many suggestions for creating *tzedakah* boxes in the first *Big Book of Great Teaching Ideas*. Before you know it, more families will be involved with filling the *tzedakah* box.

RESPECT FOR ELDERS

Celebrating Grandparents and Other Special People

Let children honor their grandparents, or if they no longer have grandparents living, have them identify someone in their family they would like to recognize: perhaps an aunt, uncle, cousin, or sibling.

Have each child create an acrostic poem using the name of the honoree. Show students an example of an acrostic, then tell them to write the person's name, vertically on the left side of a piece of paper. Using each letter as the beginning of a word, students think of a word or phrase that describes how important their honoree is to them. When students have completed the acrostic, they can copy it neatly on colorful drawing paper, leaving space for decorations or handprints. Each student then signs his or her page.

Have available large-size mailing envelopes so the pictures do not have to be folded. When they are dry, place each in a separate envelope for students to take home. Each student can personally give or mail his or her acrostic to its intended recipient. The children will have performed a mitzvah by thanking someone for being there or saying something nice about someone.

Generation to Generation

In the Talmud it says: "Rabbi ben Levi said, 'Have respect and honor for the old and saintly whose physical powers are broken, just as you would for the young and healthy; for the broken Stone Tablets, just as the whole ones, were given a place in the Holy Ark of the Covenant.'"

We often forget a very valuable resource available in most synagogues: the elderly. The children's grandparents and senior members of your congregation can make a wonderful contribution to the Jewish education of children.

Gather together grandparents and interested senior members of your congregation. Read the quote from the Talmud and explain to them that you want your students to learn to respect the elderly by establishing a relationship with them. Talk about the various activities you would like to do (some suggestions follow); be sure to get some additional ideas from them. Encourage as many elders as possible to participate and sign them up. Give them a date when the project will begin.

Now you have to prepare the children. Begin a brainstorming session by asking; "What is old?" Record children's answers on the blackboard and be sure everyone has a chance to contribute to the list. Once students are finished, read over the list and comment about someone they would know: "So-and-so is old and these words don't seem to describe him (or her) very well—it makes me wonder. . . ." See if the kids can name some other people whom they consider old and talk about how these people fit into the different words students have supplied in their brainstorming list.

For the next two class sessions, choose some stories whose main character is an older person. Two good books are: *Mrs. Katz and Tush* by Patricia Polacco (New York: Dell, 1994) and *Song and Dance Man* by Karen Ackerman (New York: Knopf, 1988). At the end of each story, ask the children to describe the elderly character. After the last story, ask the kids to create a new list based on the question, "Who is old?" I think you will find their answers will be quite different from the first list they created.

Once you have these preparatory activities, tell the students that they are going to have an opportunity to have an elder friend. Children will, of course, ask questions like How old will he or she be? What will he or she be like? When will we meet him or her? etc. Begin to prepare the kids for their first meeting with their new friends. Form small groups and have each group create a list of questions the members would like to ask an elder. Upon completion in their small groups, bring the students together to share their questions. The class then chooses five questions to ask their new friends.

For the first meeting, group together tables and chairs so that four people will sit at a table: two elders and two children. This first meeting is really a getting-to-know-you-session. Have the elders sit two to a table, across from each other; then children randomly take their seats, two to a table. The elder on the right becomes a child's friend for the year, or however long you plan to continue the project. Give the pairs some time to "discover" each other, sharing questions about who they are. Have a snack—the children can serve their new friends—and maybe have a short session where the children introduce their new friend to the rest of the class.

That is a very simple first session, but you will need to plan for the rest. Try to hold at least one meeting a month. The activities can dovetail your curriculum, a Jewish holiday that takes place during or after your session, and so on. You can also do some brainstorming with the elders and students to see what they would like to be doing together. Here is a list of some potential activities that could take place during the year:

- Have seniors share a favorite story about a Jewish holiday or event in their lives.
- Have students share how their families celebrate a specific Jewish holiday today.
- Have both groups read the same story, then come together to discuss the story and how it relates to them. Discuss the characters in the story, with students and seniors sharing their views, and then write a new ending to the story.
- Have students prepare an art gallery display for their new friends. As part of their unit of study, students draw pictures, create collages, and so on to display at their next meeting.
- Have seniors share their experiences as they were growing up. What was school like? How did they travel? What was their favorite food for the holidays? What brought them to this city? What did they do when they arrived? How did they make a living?
- Have seniors bring in a memento from their past to share. It might be an object, a family picture, a book, or it could be a memory or a story about their childhood.

This list can go on and on, but you get the idea. The important thing is to get the senior adults in your congregation involved with the religious school. They have much to offer!

OTHER VALUES AND CONCEPTS

The Hebrew Calendar

On 8½ x 11 card stock, write the names of each Hebrew month in both Hebrew and English transliteration. Include symbols of any Jewish holidays taking place during that month. Laminate or cover with clear contact paper. If necessary, repeat months so that you have one per child.

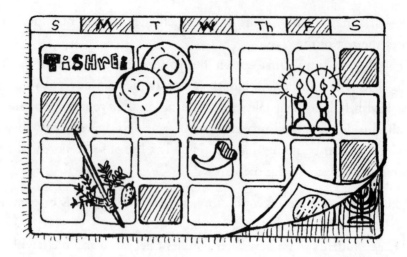

Give each child a month card. Talk about the different Hebrew months briefly, writing on the board the name of each month as you mention it. Ask the students to repeat the name of the month after you. Then say a month, pointing to it on the board and ask the child who has that month to stand and repeat the name. The student then can show the card and ask his or her classmates if they recognize any of the symbols. What holiday do the pictures represent? If no one knows, just tell students the name of the holiday. Continue until all the children have had a turn. *Note:* You can also compare the Hebrew calendar to the secular calendar. Let the children identify the Hebrew month in which their birthday takes place.

Jewish Family Traditions

Begin this lesson by telling about a tradition your own family has. For example, more than twenty years ago my family created its own Haggadah. Every two or three years we'd make some changes in it to meet the needs of the younger children in our family. Now that the grandchildren have gotten older, it is about to be changed again.

Encourage the children to talk about their own family traditions, choosing their favorites. Give them some drawing paper and markers or crayons. Have each student draw a picture of his or her favorite family tradition, label it, and make a simple frame for it. Each child then shares the pictures and tells why this family tradition is so important.

Special Presentations

Ask the children to think about an exciting Jewish event they have recently experienced. It could be a sibling's bar or bar mitzvah, a Shabbat dinner (with or without guests), a seder, a Purim party, or so on. Establish a place in the classroom where each student can design a presentation to share that special experience with the class. Provide students with creative materials to use if they desire, like construction paper, scissors, glue, glitter, buttons, and whatever else is handy.

When they have completed their creations, one at a time each child presents the story of his or her special Jewish experience. Encourage the class to ask questions of the student after his or her presentation. When all the children have made their presentations, talk about making Jewish memories. What kind of memories do they now have? You can refer to the different Jewish experiences the children have just finished describing.

The Bible and Jewish History

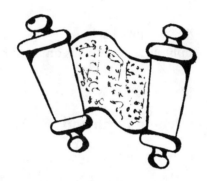

Rules: A Gentle Introduction to the Torah

Even the very young can learn why we have rules. You can use this activity as an introduction to some simple laws from the Torah.

Talk to the children briefly about rules, naming a few that they will know about, such as no running in the school hall and no pushing. Ask them to think of some other rules, guiding them as you make a list of the rules from the students. (Use this as an opportunity to review your class rules!) Talk with students about the purpose of the rules, leading them to understand that most rules help make a place safe, enjoyable, clean, and so on.

Looking at the list of rules that the children have created, choose one that corresponds to a law in the Torah. For example: "Honor your mother and father." Exodus 20:12 could be applied to a lot of rules in young children's lives. The Holiness Code in Leviticus, chapter 19, would probably be your best source. Read the law from the Torah and help students to understand the relationship between the Torah's Law and the need for laws and rules that help everyone live a better life.

Teaching Bible

A delightful little book for this age group is *Let's Play Noah's Ark* by Leon Baxter (Colorado Springs: Chariot Victor, 1995). The idea is that when you read the story, you have materials handy so the children can act out the story as it is being read. For example, different-size boxes can become "Noah's ark" for a couple of small children. Cut out pairs of the animals that will be entering the ark, or have stuffed toys for this purpose. Have umbrellas and raincoats for the rain. Include food—cookies, empty cereal boxes, food packets, and bags—to load into the ark. Be sure to prepare for the rain, too. Cut up pieces of paper or use confetti. If that is too messy, try making strips of heavy aluminum foil and rattle them (it makes a noise similar to rain), or place some rice in a box and shake it; this will sound like the rain drops are falling. Just follow the story and you will see all the different items you will need. Make it a fun time for the children as they hear the story of Noah.

This approach is just one example. You can use this approach with any of the Bible stories. Just have the appropriate materials on hand for the children to use. Be creative.

Another Approach to Teaching Noah and the Ark

Tell children the story of Noah. If you want, use a picture book or the actual text from the Torah. Have all kinds of art materials available, along with shoe boxes and large plastic bottles that can be used for arks. In addition, have either animal stencils or stickers for the children to use.

Divide the class into small groups of two to three children. Each group is to create its own ark. When the groups have completed their work, review the story. The children can compare their work to what the story says, making any additions or corrections to their arks as needed. Then, each group displays its work and explains its work of art.

The Garden of Eden

Give the children an opportunity to use their imaginations! Read a story about the Garden of Eden or some of the actual text from the Torah, being as visual as possible. Have ready all kinds of creative art materials for students to use, including construction and tissue paper, pipe cleaners, markers, crayons, felt, foil, scissors, glue, and so on. Now encourage students to think about what the Garden of Eden might have looked like. Invite children to actually create their own Garden of Eden. Give them time to complete it (and time for everyone to ooh and ahh over one another's work). Ask each child to explain his or her creation. Display the projects on the wall or make a bulletin board, using all of their creative work.

A Potpourri of Ideas

These activities can be used for just about any subject matter.

A Time for Sharing

Send home a letter to parents telling them the class is going to be studying the impact of Jewish artifacts on their lives. Ask the students to talk to their parents about a Jewish item they have in their house that has special memories or the oldest Jewish artifact they have in the house. This will give the parents a chance to tell a story to their children as they identify the item. Choose a day for children to bring these special Jewish items to school. Invite each child to show the item and tell its story and about his or her parents' special Jewish memory. Discuss with the students how Jewish artifacts can reveal information about their personal Jewish history. Each student then writes about his or her Jewish artifact and draws a picture of it. Create a bulletin board which displays all their Jewish artifacts.

Story Questions

After reading or telling a story to your class, ask children a series of questions to stimulate some thought about the story or a specific character, for example: Who did what? How did so-and-so react?

When a child answers thoughtfully, let him or her act out what the character did. Do this for the different characters in the story, with emphasis on the major Jewish concepts and values found within the story.

Story Envelopes

Divide the class into small groups. Prepare "story envelopes" by placing up to ten words on 3 x 5 index cards or colorful strips of paper. Make enough so that each group has its own story envelope. Groups are to create a short story using all the words from their envelope. Upon completion, they share their stories with the class.

Children Create Their Own Storybooks

This activity will take more than one session, but the end result will be worth the effort. You might need parents or aides to help those students that are non-writers. Divide the class into small groups. Have on hand several Jewish-themed picture books. Show the books to the children, identifying the different parts: cover, title page, dedication, text, and illustrations.

Now, place on the board a list of potential titles the children can use for their own storybooks. The children might want to add subjects of their own based on their personal experiences. That's fine as long as the content covers some aspect of Judaism.

Give the groups time to talk about their stories and to create brief outlines. They can also discuss the kind of illustrations they will need and what they will use to create their artwork: crayons, markers, watercolors, or pencils.

In another session, have each group write the first draft of its story. Have each group share the writing. The class then works together to edit the story, suggesting changes. (Remind children to make their comments in a positive manner.) The group rewrites its story based on this input.

During the concluding session children finalize their stories, complete the artwork, design the cover and title page, and write the dedication. They then assemble the books. The finished books can be placed in the library.

Paper Strips

On small, colorful paper strips, write one-sentence situations. This approach works for just about any subject matter but lends itself particularly well to stories about Bible, holidays, and Jewish concepts and values. Your sentences could look something like this:

> Joseph was thrown into a pit.
> Mother lit the candles.
> Aviva brought three cans of tuna to school.

Place the strips into a large bag or box. Assign students partners; each pair then draws one strip from the bag or box. After reading their strip, children determine the who, what, where, when, why, and how questions relevant to the situation. Take the sentence "Joseph was thrown into a pit," for example. Questions might include the following: Where did this take place? How did this happen? Why was Joseph treated in this manner? Once they have come up with their questions, students are to write the answers to them. Upon completion, the partners share with the class both the questions and the answers.

Numbered Pictures

Choose a picture that fits in with your unit of study. Lay a piece of tracing paper over it. Place dots on the outline of the picture. Number the dots in the order the students are to follow. Copy the tracing paper. Students follow the dots, then color it in. Ask them to identify the picture and explain what they know.

Creating Mazes

You do not need to depend on someone else to create mazes—you can easily create them yourself, and the kids love them. Many of these also exist as handouts in various activity workbooks. Some examples of what you can do:

A maze that takes students from Jerusalem to Tel Aviv.
One that takes Jonah through the stomach of the whale to be redeemed.
Another that takes the students on a trip to find the hidden *afikoman*.

Give it a try—it is fun!

Puppet Shows

Have some fun with your studies. Let the students create different puppets. Each puppet is to represent one person they have encountered in their studies. Let small groups of children come together and create a skit that involves their puppets. Even the youngest can be involved in this kind of activity. Give them time to practice, then on with the show!

News Headlines

After studying a portion of your unit of study, give students five or six headlines based on the unit. Students are to briefly describe the news behind the headlines. They could even create a newspaper using the headlines to write their articles for the paper. Or, after a section of study, ask the students to write five or six headlines that best describe what they just studied.

Illustrate a Story

Choose a story the children will like and that teaches a Jewish value or concept. Ask the children to listen very carefully because they are going to be asked to draw pictures to go with the story. Write one or two sentences on blank sheets of paper, and give each child a different page. Then ask the children to draw the illustrations to go with the story. When all the illustrations are complete, compile the book and copy so each child has a book to take home.

"I Spy"

Place a variety of Jewish items (or pictures of objects) on the table, all based on your unit of study. Look at the table and in your mind pick an object; think about it, then tell the students "I spy." The students can ask five "yes" or "no" questions about the object to guess what it is. Then let the kids have their turn, one at a time.

Make a Jewish Wind Sock

You will need a paper lunch bag for each student, brightly colored crepe paper cut into strips, glue, and pipe cleaners. Cut the bottom quarter off each lunch bag and give one to each student. Ask the students to write words and then to draw pictures or cut out pictures that represent your subject matter. Children are to decorate all four sides of the bag. Give each student a bunch of the strips of colored crepe paper and have them glue the strips *inside* of the bag, all around. Punch two holes in the top of the bag and help the students thread a pipe cleaner through the holes for a handle. Hang the wind socks around the room to make it more colorful, or let students take them home and hang them outside on a windy (but not rainy!) day.

Alternative
Make use of old posters, or let the students create new ones based on a Jewish concept from your unit of study.

Take the poster and laminate or cover with clear contact paper—especially if it is going to be hung outside. Roll the poster up and staple it in the shape of a tube. At one end, punch three holes spaced evenly apart. Thread yarn or string through these holes to be able to hang the wind sock. At the other end, glue or staple streamers of crepe paper, ribbon, yarn, or scraps of material (cut into strips with pinking shears so they won't unravel). Hang the wind socks around your room or outside your classroom window.

Intermediate Grades

Children in the intermediate grades are great to teach. They are still a challenge to the educator; they want to learn, but the teacher has to be on his or her toes to keep up with them. This is even more so in today's world. Intermediate-grade students are smart and like to be entertained—so entertain them with creative teaching ideas!

Jewish Holidays

SHABBAT

Advertising Sells!

Have students prepare an advertising campaign for a brand-new design for Shabbat ritual objects including candlesticks, challah cover, *Kiddush* cup, *Havdalah* set, and so on.

Divide the class into small groups. Each group is to design the most unique and creative Shabbat ritual objects possible. Have the students create explicit pictures of their new product, as well as a written description and a slogan or musical jingle. Then have each group plan an advertising campaign, deciding on the kind of customer who will purchase the object and the media the group will advertise in (radio, television, print). Have the group also decide the price of the object. (Or, students could even decide that they will give their ritual objects free to each family who promises to use them to celebrate Shabbat each week!) Set aside time for each group to make its presentation using whatever forms of media were chosen.

Shabbat Story

Have children write short stories of how they celebrate Shabbat. Or, divide the class into small groups. Assign each group a different country where Jews live and have children write a collective short story about how Shabbat is celebrated in that country. Provide library time or reference books or prepare readings for the students to help them gain this information. Share students' stories with the class and then compile all the stories into a booklet for everyone to take home.

Picture Shabbat

This will take a little effort, but it is worth it. It is really an introduction to a more in-depth study of Shabbat. Gather together a large number of magazines. Go through the magazines and cut out pictures that you think represent the "essence" of Shabbat. Concepts might include the following:

> *M'nuchah*—Shabbat rest
> *Oneg Shabbat*—joy of the Sabbath
> *T'filah*—Shabbat worship
> *Mishpachah*—family togetherness
> *Shalom*—Shabbat peace

You will need enough pictures for the class to be divided into groups of three or four and each group will share five pictures. Once you have all the pictures, glue each picture to a large index card. Also have available: colorful strips of paper (two or three per student), felt-tip markers, and masking tape.

Pass out two or three colorful strips of paper and a felt-tip marker to each student. Talk about the meaning of Shabbat. As you talk, take one of the strips of paper and a marker, and tell the students: "To me, Shabbat is peace." Write this on your strip of paper and post it on the wall. Then, ask the students to write one word which comes to mind when they say "To me, Shabbat is . . ." Give them time to do two or three. Let them post their strips on the wall after they share their ideas with the class. If you use different colored strips of paper, it becomes an attractive, colorful wall explaining students' ideas about Shabbat.

Now, place the index cards face down on a table. Explain to the students that often when we look at pictures we each will see something different—just as we each view Shabbat in a different way. Tell students they will find on the cards pictures that contain some "essence" of Shabbat. Take a few pictures to show children, giving them an example of how you yourself see Shabbat in the pictures. Tell the students to gather in groups and each group takes five cards. Allow time for them to do so. As students look at the pictures, each individual is to decide which ones come closest to his or her idea of Shabbat and what it means to them. They might look at the picture and think: "To me, Shabbat is like this picture because . . ."

After each individual has written on his or her groups' cards, the group will discuss what ideas are similar in the group. Then the groups will create:

1. A name for their group.
2. A symbol for their group.
3. A slogan for their group.

If time allows, encourage the group to write a poem or song which tells about members' ideas. Then, students share their creativity with the whole class.

HIGH HOLY DAYS

Challah as a High Holy Days Symbol

We are familiar with the customs of dipping apples in honey for a sweet year; eating fish, which symbolize fruitfulness; and eating lamb to remind us of Isaac's sacrifice. We find a challah on our table for all our holidays, but on the High Holy Days the challah has a different shape. Numbers 15:18–21 states: "When you enter the land into which I will bring you and when you eat of the bread of the land, you shall present an offering to the Lord. You shall offer a cake of the first of your dough . . . throughout your generations." Since priestly offerings can no longer be made, and in order that this mitzvah may not be forgotten, we are bidden to throw a small portion of the challah dough (the size of an olive) into the fire.

During the High Holy Days, we use a round challah, which symbolizes the cycle of life, time, and the year itself. The shape also conveys the idea that just as a circle has no end or beginning, so is God Eternal, without beginning or end. Because we generally no longer bake bread ourselves, it is now customary to set aside something for *tzedakah* in conjunction with the "removal of challah."

For this activity, prepare a sheet on which you draw a round challah from three distinct circles, with the bottom one the biggest, the middle a little smaller, and the top smaller still—a crown for the challah. Make sure it looks like a round challah viewed from the side or the top. In each row, draw lines to create sections in which the students can draw or write their responses.

Have the students fill in the circles as follows:

- Row 1: Write the life-cycle events that have taken place within your family and that will occur sometime in the future.
- Row 2: Make a list of acts of loving-kindness you can do to help other people in the coming year.
- Row 3: This is the crown of the challah, which represents the crown or glory of God. Identify those things for which you would praise God.

Upon completion, students share their ideas with the entire class.

TU BISH'VAT ACTIVITIES

Taking Care of Our Earth

Here are a variety of activities to help the children become aware of the Jewish aspects of taking care of our earth:

1. Have a conversation with the earth. If students could talk to the earth, what would it say in return?
2. Talk about how to heal the earth. What makes it our responsibility as Jews to save the earth?
3. Gather together pictures that show the beauty (and the ugliness) of the earth. Place the pictures in a

large bag. One at a time, blindfold each child and have him or her draw a picture out of the bag. Then, have each student write a poem or story to go with the picture. Compile a book of children's work, or mount the picture and writing on construction paper and hang on the walls. You could even arrange to display students' work throughout the synagogue.

4. Gather together quotes from Jewish sources which have to do with preservation of the earth, all aspects of it. Place each quote on a separate piece of paper. Blindfold each child, one at a time, and have him or her draw one quote from the bag. Based on their quote, the students are to draw and illustrate, or create a poster that goes with the quote. Display their completed work.

PURIM

The biggest complaint about Purim I always hear from the kids is "We've studied this before!" And they are more than likely right. The following activities are designed for students who already know something about Purim. If they say they know so much, find out how much they do know! What they *don't* know becomes your lesson.

Similarities and Differences: Purim and Chanukah

Have the students mentally review what they know about Chanukah and Purim. On the board place two columns, one for Chanukah and one for Purim. Then ask questions like:

When do the holidays occur?
Who are the villains?
Who are the heroes?
What was the miracle?
Where did the miracle occur?
When did the miracle take place?
How is each miracle commemorated today?
How do we reach out to others on these days?
Whom do we involve in the celebration?

Letters to Vashti

Students enjoy this activity because it is different from the usual Purim activities. Encourage students to use their sense of humor as they engage in it.

Have students write letters to Vashti. They can give Vashti encouragement to stand by her decision or warn her not to be too hasty—it's their choice. Have students read the first two chapters of the *M'gillah* to understand the queen's status in court with reference to the king and the empire.

As they prepare to write their letters to Vashti, invite students to imagine themselves as a person from that time period. Some suggested roles are:

Jewish woman living in Persia
Leader of the Persian Jewish community
Local merchant in Persia
Mordechai
Biblical prophet

If they wish it, allow students to work in pairs (sometimes two heads are better than one). After they have finished, have students read aloud their letters and discuss how convincing the letters were.

YOM HAATZMA-UT

You are There

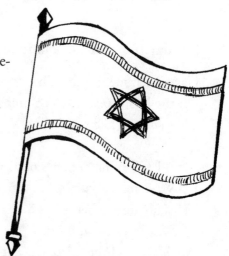

With a little planning, this can become a grade-wide or even a whole-school activity. Set up a number of stations, with a different activity in each one, and enlist the aid of parents or volunteers to head the stations. Divide students into groups and have the groups rotate through the various stations. Tell students they are to imagine they are back in Israel in 1948.

- *Israeli flag:* Students work together to create their own Israeli flag using different Jewish symbols. Remember this is 1948, before Israel chose a flag. The person who runs the station could ask the kids to imagine they are an Israeli Betsy Ross, and they need to create a flag for their new country.

- *The Haganah:* Tell the students they are members of the Haganah (the pre-Israeli army). The group is moving from one place to another with an injured soldier—and is confronted by British soldiers. What should the students do?
- *Israel Information Jeopardy:* Play just like the game on TV. Some suggestions for categories: Cities, Historical Sites, How Do You Say It in Hebrew?, History, Famous People.
- *Desert Irrigation:* Water is vital to Israel. Tell the kids they need to get water to the Negev. Yes, the old spoon and water trick! Have handy a pail of water and a spoon, and place a small plastic cup twenty or so feet away (the Negev). Kids have to fill the cup! Don't forget the paper towels!
- *History Time Line:* Create a time line of Israel's history up to this point. Use pictures and stories, and have the station leader walk each group through the time line.
- *Build the Kotel:* You'll need lots of shoe boxes for bricks. Have each group build a section of the Wall. Try to have enough boxes so the Wall could be left standing for a while so people can write notes and insert them into the Wall. Perhaps a congregation member going to Israel would be willing to bring the notes and place them in the actual *Kotel.*

Conclude the program by bringing the group together for a song session. Provide song sheets if necessary. Be sure to include "Hatikvah."

All About Cities Activity Book

Divide the class into small groups. Assign each group a different city in Israel. Each group is to find out as much as it can about the particular location. If necessary, have the class visit the library, or provide sources for students to use. After the students have finished their research, the groups are to come up with two or three activity sheets that will disseminate the information. Some possible ideas are:

- *Hidden words:* Make up a word search using words related to the city. For example, a word search about Haifa might include "Mount Carmel," "Baha'i," and "port."
- *Dot-to-dot pictures:* Using tracing paper, outline a picture with dots and number them in the order you want the outline drawn. It should be something of major interest for the location—King David's Tower in Jerusalem, for example.

- *Maze:* Draw a maze that begins at one place and ends up in a specific location. As students "travel" through the maze, they can visit sites along the way that are found in the city.
- *Map of Israel:* Have blank maps of Israel and a list of places you want students to locate. As they locate each site, they mark the place on the map. (You may wish to provide this page yourself, making sure that—at the very least—each assigned city is included on the map.)
- *Crossword puzzle:* Create a crossword puzzle that when completed will tell the groups something about the city.
- *Word scrambles:* These are always fun. Make up a list of words about your location and then scramble the words. The groups have to unscramble and identify each one.

When the students have finished, combine all the activities into a booklet and make a copy for each student. They will have fun completing the various sheets and learn something at the same time!

Celebration of Israel

This is a way to involve all the classes in a grade. You'll need to get some aides or parent volunteers to help out. Also, it's a good idea to coordinate your activities with your school's music specialist, if there is one.

You'll need to create at least four stations. Mix up the classes to create four groups (and to give students in the same grade but different classes a chance to mingle). The number of groups should be the same as the number of stations. The groups rotate around each station for a fixed, short period of time. Here are some suggestions for stations:

- *Singing:* What would a celebration of Israel be without a sing-along? Choose some songs, make up song sheets to distribute, decorate them, and just sing out!
- *Israeli dancing:* No handouts for this one, but everyone can learn at least one dance during the program. Just imagine if students all learn the same dance in small groups! A grand closure for the program could be everyone dancing together at the end.
- *Israeli foods:* Have the kids, with adult help, create a falafel sandwich. Have the ingredients for the sandwiches—the pita, hummus, falafel, and salad—prepared in advance. During the program, children can have a snack of falafel sandwiches.

- *Next year in Jerusalem:* Have each group write a collective poem about some aspect of Israel. At the end of the program, groups read their poems aloud.
- *Make an Israeli flag:* Have materials available so students can make a flag to take home.
- *Pin the flag on Jerusalem:* Any takeoff on pin the tail on the donkey is always popular with young students.
- *Archaeological dig:* It's always fun to dig in the sand. Just hide all kind of artifacts for the kids to find.

With advance preparation, this can be a great all-session activity. You may even wish to invite parents to participate as well. Just have children create invitations to send home in advance.

ACTIVITIES FOR ANY HOLIDAY

Holiday Matchup

On the left-hand side of a sheet of paper, list some words or statements that have to do with your holiday. Then write the corresponding explanations of the words or statements out of order on the right-hand side of the paper. For example, for Purim, your list could look something like this:

Adar	Scroll of Esther
Ahashuerus	Purim play
Al Hanisim	Celebrated in walled cities
Esther	Sending of gifts
Haman	Queen of Persia before Esther
hamantashen	Twelfth month of Jewish year
M'gillat Esther	"For the miracles"
mishlo-ach manot	Ahasuerus's vizier
Mordecai	Also know as Hadassah
Purimshpiel	triangular pastries
Shushan Purim	The king of Persia
Vashti	Esther's cousin

Students match the words to the corresponding definitions by drawing a line from the list on the left to the list on the right.

Holiday Multiple Choice

Make this a game and decorate the sheet you prepare with pictures and drawings. Prepare a list of multiple-choice questions for the students based on the holiday you are studying. Split the students into groups and turn this into a competitive quiz game with prizes for everyone. What follows are some of my ideas for Purim, but you can come up with some of your own for Purim and any other holiday:

1. In what city did the story of Purim take place?
    a. Shushan
    b. Tehran
    c. Jerusalem
2. Where is this city located today?
    a. Egypt
    b. Israel
    c. Iran
3. What was the name of the king's wife before Esther?
    a. Sarah
    b. Rebecca
    c. Vashti
4. What was Esther's other name?
    a. Rivkah
    b. Hadassah
    c. Yehudit
5. Why was Haman angry at Mordecai?
    a. Mordecai didn't want to come to Haman's party.
    b. Mordechai refused to kneel down to Haman.
    c. Mordechai owed Haman money.
6. What saved the Jewish people from Haman's evil decree?
    a. Vashti apologized to Ahasuerus.
    b. Haman was voted out of office.
    c. Esther told Ahasuerus about it.
7. What do hamantashen symbolize?
    a. Haman's shoes
    b. Haman's hat
    c. Shushan's three corners
8. What are *mishlo-ach manot*?
    a. Esther's beautiful dresses
    b. The rivers in Shushan
    c. Baskets of food given to friends and the needy on Purim

9. What does *Pur* mean?
   a. Lots
   b. Let's eat!
   c. Haman's coat
10. What is a *s'udah?*
   a. A purim costume
   b. A festive meal
   c. A minor festival

Top Ten Lists for the Holidays

David Letterman's Top Ten lists have become a staple on his talk show. For a fun activity, let your students create their own. Divide the class into small groups. For example, each group is to list the "Top Ten Reasons to Celebrate Purim." Or the "Top Ten Plagues" (for Pesach) or the "Top Ten Commandments" (for Shavuot) and so on. Feel free to come up with your own and be as funny as possible. Each group presents its list, beginning with item 10. Maybe there will be a few laughs.

Funny Stories for the Holidays

Divide the class into small groups. Gather together five or six short, humorous stories from Jewish stories or midrashim. Give each group a different set of stories. Ask the groups to read through the stories and choose the one story they think is the funniest. Once they have selected a story, students are to create a short skit that tells the story. Give students time to rehearse, then let them present their skits to the whole class. The class can even decide which one was the funniest. However, to be sure everyone wins, have additional categories: the silliest, the most serious, and so on. Have some ribbons to award to the different groups for their efforts and for winning!

Holiday Book

This is good for any holiday and is an excellent closure to a lesson. You will need supplies that include the following:

Blank paper of various colors
Ruled paper
Pencils, crayons, and markers

Glue, stapler, tape, and scissors
Small pictures related to the holiday
Old magazines that can be cut up

After you have studied a specific holiday, ask the students to create a book about the holiday. They can work individually, or you can divide the class into pairs or small groups. Tell them they can write stories, draw pictures, and create games and puzzles to include in their holiday book. Encourage children to be creative and to think about what they will include. To spur them on, you might ask questions such as the following (not all questions apply to every holiday):

How was the holiday celebrated in the past?
How is it celebrated today?
How would you celebrate the holiday in the future?
What traditional foods are usually eaten?
What foods would you like to eat today for the holiday?
What symbols and rituals belong with this holiday?
Where in the Bible does it tell us to celebrate this holiday?
How does the Bible tell us to celebrate the holiday?

When students are ready, let them choose the materials they will use. Remind children to design a cover and a title page. Students share the completed books with one another, then each child can bring his or hers home. If more than one student created a given book, make copies so each child can take a book home.

Create a Jewish Holiday Cookbook

Food is an important element of each holiday. There are certain foods that we eat and enjoy. Regardless of the age of your students, it would be a challenge for them to research the different foods eaten for each holiday. They could even include the special foods eaten by Ashkenazic and Sephardic Jews in different countries.

The fun part would be to collect the same recipes and create a Jewish holiday cookbook from around the world! Encourage children to ask their parents, grandparents, relatives, and friends for recipes.

Be sure to include the name of the person who has contributed the recipe. Compile their efforts and copy so each student has a cookbook to take home. Make a few extra copies to place in the synagogue library.

Bring some cookbooks to class to get the students started. Three excellent cookbooks that can be used for research are *Jewish Cooking in America* and *The Jewish Holiday Kitchen* both by Joan Nathan and *The Book of Jewish Food: An Odyssey from Samarkand to New York* by Claudia Roden.

Shoe Box Jewish Holidays

This is a little different. You will need one shoe box for each group of students. Prepare on index cards five questions for each holiday. Place the cards into a box, a different box for each holiday. Have a supply of decorating materials and books for research available.

Divide the class into small groups. Give each group a "shoe box holiday box." Explain that the group is to find the answers to all the holiday questions in the box, then decorate the box to represent that holiday. To conclude, each group presents its completed holiday box to the class, with students explaining the decorations and sharing all they have learned about the holiday.

Books for the Lower Grades

Give your older students an opportunity to perform a mitzvah! As part of their review of a holiday, have students create short, simple stories for young children. Students can research the answers and then create the book. Encourage them to creatively illustrate the books. *Note:* You may wish to play to students' strengths by dividing up the researching, writing, and illustrating tasks.

Holiday Contest

This is a good way to review the holidays. Prepare review questions on holiday cutouts, using symbols that are related to the holidays. On each cutout place a point value, then hide the cutouts around the room.

Create some simple rules to the game. Some rules could be: students cannot ask the teacher any questions; students can look in their books for answers; and students can work in pairs. Set a time limit to find and answer all the questions. The team with the most value points at the end of the time period will be the winner.

Holiday Lists

Here's another way to review holidays. Prepare index cards with the name of a Jewish holiday on each card. The students can work individually or in pairs to make "quick lists" of everything they can remember about their holiday. They choose a card, then make their list. The students with the longest list of correct facts will be the winners.

Holiday *Tzedakah*

Most Jewish holidays have some sort of *tzedakah* component. To help your students make the connection, design your lesson so the *tzedakah* activity is incorporated into the curriculum for the holiday. Some advance preparation will be necessary. First contact a homeless shelter, group home, or other agency to determine what it needs. Identify a time period during which students can collect items and arrange for the agency to pick up and distribute them. (Or, arrange for students, accompanied by adults, to deliver goods personally.) Send a letter home to each family explaining the project and elicit parents' cooperation.

A few examples of what you could do:

- Sukkot: Donate fruits and vegetables to a food kitchen.
- Chanukah: Collect light bulbs, bottles of vegetable oil, baby oil, and lotion to be distributed to shelters and food banks.
- Tu BiSh'vat: Donate house plants to shelters and group homes.
- Lag BaOmer: Collect magazines, sporting goods, and books. Donate to homeless shelters or to children's homes and hospitals.

Design a New Jewish Holiday

This is a good way to review the Jewish holidays. With the kids, make a list of all the Jewish holidays. Be sure to include Rosh Chodesh (just in case they think of creating a holiday to celebrate the New Moon). Include those holidays students might not know too much about, like Lag BaOmer or Tishah B'Av. Review what these days celebrate and briefly explain how they are celebrated. Now, do some brainstorming so the kids can come up with some ideas for new Jewish holidays. When students think the list is complete, divide them into small groups and let each group choose one of the potential new holidays. Tell children to think about how our Jewish holidays are celebrated, what symbols are used, what foods are eaten, what special prayers are said, and so on. Then, let the kids go and create their celebrations. Upon completion, they share with the whole class.

Holiday Bookmarks

You'll need felt, cardstock or ribbon, and fabric glue. Out of the felt, cut two Jewish symbols for each student. (If they can, let students cut them out themselves.) Cut the ribbon or card stock into 2 x 10 strips, one per student. Using the fabric glue, place the card stock or ribbon between the two Jewish symbols and glue the symbols together. The students can decorate the ribbon or card stock in any manner they wish.

Jewish Identity

Who Is Coming to Dinner?

Tell the students they are allowed to invite three famous Jews to dinner. Guests can be living or dead, from the distant past or in the here and now. Students must describe who their guests are and the reason for inviting them. This helps students make connections between themselves and the Jewish people as a whole.

What Would You Wish For?

Tell the students they have been granted three wishes: one for the students, one for the family, and one for the community or world. Children are to describe their wishes and the reasons for making them. This helps students consider what values are important to them. Then relate the values that are important to them to Jewish values.

Greeting the Aliens

Ask students to pretend that they are going on a spaceship to Mars. Life has been found there, and the class is going to meet these new aliens. Before they leave, students must create greeting cards that tell these aliens something about Jews. What do we want them to know? How will students describe themselves? How can students show the aliens that Jews are very friendly people? What kind of pictures can students use?

Give the students some scrap paper so they can begin drafting their greeting cards. From time to time, remind students to tell about themselves and about the Jewish people and religion. When each student has satisfactorily finished his or her draft, give out some 8½ x 11 card stock and colored pencils, markers, or crayons. Have each student draw his or her finished greeting on the card stock and decorate with pictures or as desired. Encourage students to share their greeting cards. Talk about what the students have placed on their cards. Have students answered all the questions raised? What do they think the aliens will learn about Jews and Judaism from the greeting cards? What else might be needed? This will give the kids some food for thought as to who they are as Jews right now.

Stories from Home

What's in the bag? Give each student a ziploc bag to take home. Explain to them they must bring it back with eight to ten small items or pictures that represent who they are as a Jew, or collectively who they are as a Jewish family.

When students return with their filled bags, the fun part begins. Collect the bags and give one to each student. Be sure a student does not get his or her own bag! Tell the students they are to write a story incorporating five or six items from the bag. The story should explain the author's Jewish identity. Upon completion, the students share the results. When a student has finished telling his or her story, ask the bag's owner: "How close did the other student come to the description of your Jewish identity?" The results could be interesting.

What's in a Jewish Name?

Ask each student to find out what his or her Hebrew name is. How was it selected? After whom is the student named? Give students some time to gather this information.

Next, either plan a class visit to the library or bring in some naming books. Tell the students to find out first what their Hebrew name means and then what their English name means. (Some English names go back a long way and have special meanings.) Students can compare the meanings of their Hebrew and English names.

Now have students consider whom they were named after. In what way does the description of the person relate to the meaning of the student's name? What virtues, characteristics, and Jewish values did that person have? How does the student relate to this person? Does the student have some of the same virtues or characteristics?

Have available scratch paper and pencils. Ask each student first to design a symbol that reflects the meaning of his or her Hebrew name, and then to create a logo using the symbol. Once the student is satisfied with the logo, give out card stock and markers. Let students draw the logo design on the card stock. Place the logos around the room and have each student explain to the class how the design represents the distinctiveness of his or her Hebrew name.

The Bible and Jewish History

Jewish Text Comes Alive!

This activity, which has been adapted from one written by Harlene Appelman, is a prime example of how to make Jewish text come alive for the students. They will not only understand it, they will relate the text to life today. Use the verses from *Parashat Vayeira,* in which Abraham hastens to greet the three visitors to his tent, not only making them welcome but offering them food as well (Genesis 18:1–8).

After reading the text, ask: What is the hardest thing to do when welcoming guests into your home? What is the easiest thing to do? What are your biggest challenges for being a good guest? Which is more fun, to be a host or to be a guest?

Point out that sometimes it is difficult to figure out what is the proper thing to do as a guest in someone else's home, just as it is sometimes difficult to welcome guests into your own home. Have the class do some brainstorming to make a list of all the things that a proper guest needs to do. Then have students make a second list that details all the things a proper host needs to do to make his or her guests feel welcome. Invite students to add any special customs or rituals they themselves have for welcoming guests and making them feel comfortable. Combine the three lists—the two they developed by brainstorming and what they do at home.

Divide the lists into related sections, for example, "On Entering the Home" or "During the Meal." Then, divide the class into small groups. Assign a different section to each group. The group will create a portion of an etiquette booklet that will help both guests and hosts act appropriately. When all the groups have finished, compile all the sections and review the text in its entirety. Make any necessary additions or corrections. To make the booklet extra special, consider typing it on the computer, using elegant (but readable) fonts. Make copies for each student to take home and place one in the library for everyone to see.

Review Without a Test!

Tic-tac-toe provides a great way to review, and it's fun! Instead of using *x* or *o*, use symbols such as Jewish stars and shofars. Prepare a series of questions based on your unit of study. For example, if you want to review the story of Jacob and Esau, your questions might include the following:

Who was born first?
What did Esau take for his birthright?
Who helped Jacob deceive his father?
Which brother was a student?
Which brother loved the outdoors?
Where did Jacob go after he received Esau's birthright?
How long did Jacob work to marry his first wife?
Who was his first wife?

Place each question on 3 x 5 index cards; create many more than nine questions (for the nine tic-tac-toe squares) per game.

To play the game, divide the class into even teams. Shuffle the quiz cards well and place facedown. A student picks a card. If the student answers the question correctly, that team places its mark in one of the tic-tac-toe squares. If the question is answered incorrectly, that team misses its turn. Continue playing until one team gets three in a row.

An Introduction to the Laws of the Torah

Ask students to pretend the class is going to the planet Mulvania (or some such strange name) to create a new colony. While traveling in our spaceship the colonists—students—must consider what laws will be needed in their new home.

Divide the class into small groups. Ask each group to create three laws for the settlers of the new colony. While children are discussing and creating their laws, create a chart that will have a law heading each column. Subdivide each column into "yes" and "no" squares. Write the children's names down the far left column.

Once the groups have decided on their three proposed laws, the students then share the laws with the class, giving the reasons for their choices. Each group writes its proposed laws on the chart. Then, have the children vote "yes" or "no" on the proposed laws by coloring in the appropriate square.

Discuss the results and compare the winning laws with some of the laws from the Torah and with laws they know of in their community. Relate the activity to the Israelites' Exodus from Egypt and the need for laws to govern the freed slaves.

Extending the Fifth Commandment

Regardless of the age of the student, it would be nice to spend at least one lesson on recognizing those they love. One of the Ten Commandments says to "honor your father and mother." But it could also mean to honor those you love.

Do some brainstorming with the students, making a list of all the different things that those they love do for them. Make another list of all the things they can do to show their love and respect to those they love. On scratch paper, ask the students to create an acrostic by placing down the left side any of these words: Mother, Father, Friend, Relative, and so on. Next to each letter, students are to place a word beginning with that letter from the list they made of how they can show their love and respect, or they can use words describing their feelings. Give each student a piece of nice drawing paper on which to write the acrostic in an attractive manner. Decorate as desired. Students now have created their own cards for the ones they love.

Spin the Wheel

Use this spinner game to reinforce a lesson or help students learn different portions of the Bible. They will also learn how to look up different Torah portions.

Make a large circle—possibly cut from oak tag. Locate the center of the circle and draw spokes out from the center to the outside. The space between each spoke should be wide enough for you to write biblical citations, for example: Ruth 1:16, Genesis 15:21, or Isaiah 5:1. You can randomly select verses, or choose those with a similar theme. You can have students find references to the different holidays and how they are to be celebrated. Use your imagination, because this little game has all sorts of possibilities! Once you have all the spaces filled, punch a hole in the center and attach a spinner with a brass fastener. Make sure the spinner moves easily.

The game can be played in teams or small groups. If the latter, have enough spinning wheels so each group has its own. Get yourself a kitchen timer and determine for how long you will allow each student to search for a given reference. Make sure students understand the time limitation. How much time you allow will depend on how well you know your students. Allow enough time for them to be successful in their search, but still be challenged. As they get more proficient in searching through the Bible, you can reduce the time limit.

Aliens on the Beach!

Is there life on Mars? Who cares? But what if an alien creature were found on earth? What would students do?

Ask students to imagine that they are on a field trip to the beach to see the wonders of God's Creation. As students are looking around they find a colony of alien creatures hidden behind some dunes. At first the children are frightened, but then they realize the creatures are actually friendly. They discover that in addition to English, the aliens also speak another language that the kids do not understand. That other language is used most of the time except when the aliens are talking to the students. The aliens also eat different foods, and there are some foods they are forbidden to eat. The aliens practice a religion unknown to the students and observe different holidays. After spending some time with the aliens, the students return home. Naturally, they tell their parents about the discovery. The parents, unfortunately, do not have the same open minds of the children, and they report the discovery to the police. The police and the military go out and surround the colony of aliens to be sure they can't escape. Now the government is in a dilemma—what should be done? Many officials want to destroy the aliens and exterminate them completely, while others just want to keep them segregated in their own little ghetto.

Now ask the class to become the government! It must decide what to do with the aliens. The "officials" are to plan a course of action. What would be best for the surrounding communities? If you wish, divide the class into smaller groups. Give the groups time to map out a strategy, then bring the groups together to share their plans. Once they have shared their plans, *stop the action!*

Discuss with the students what is happening here. Has this ever happened before? To whom did it happen? What was the outcome? The "events" in this activity can be compared to various times in the history of the Jews. It can introduce a unit on the Holocaust or a lesson on anti-Semitism. Students can compare the differences and similarities between what has happened to the Jewish people in the past and what is taking place with the colony of aliens. This is a creative way to get students interested in Jewish history. Have fun with it!

Current Jewish Events

There is no reason why even younger children can't be aware of what is taking place in the world. Gather, on a regular basis, short news articles that are of Jewish interest. Each week, give two or three children a chance to prepare "news flashes." Together, have them read the article, write a brief summary of the information, then draw an illustration of the event. Students can even do this part at home on the Internet with their parents' help and bring the information to school the following week. To make their "reporting" more realistic and fun for the kids, cut up and decorate a large cardboard box to look like a television set. When they are ready, children sit inside the "television" and present their news flashes.

There Are Heroes Out There!

With the students, develop a list of criteria that make a person a hero. Begin the lesson by identifying some Jewish heroes from both past and present. How do these people fit the criteria? Have available to students a number of newspapers and magazines. Conduct a "Hero Hunt" to see how many heroes students can find as they look through the reading material. Students then each choose a hero and write one sentence that tells why this person is a hero. This helps students realize that there are people out there who are doing good things in spite of whatever conditions might exist.

Alternative

How about a mural of heroes? After the students have identified the characteristics of a hero, talk about some people they know who have these attributes. How do these people act? Encourage students to draw on their personal experiences. Point out that those people who simply do their jobs to the best of their ability can be considered heroic.

When students have identified some heroic actions, place a large piece of white butcher paper on the wall. Be sure there is plenty of space for each student to work. Have each student create a section of the mural showing people acting heroically. Children can either draw the pictures or cut them from magazines to make a collage.

Who Is This?

Use pictures of famous Jews from the past to create a guessing game. You can even use famous Jews of today and teach some current events as part of Jewish history taking place today.

Gather together some pictures of famous Jews. Include a few pictures of famous Jews who might be familiar to the students—this way children will encounter one or two that they know right off the bat! Enlarge the pictures if necessary. Copy and mount on card stock, then laminate or cover with clear contact paper. Prepare some clues for each picture and write them on the reverse side. Show the students one picture at a time and give one clue as to who it is. Give them some time to guess, then give another clue and have them guess again, continuing until they have identified the person. Do a few more, but stop when interest in the game has dwindled or you have accomplished your goal.

Alternative
Let each student choose a picture of a person and develop the clues. Each student presents his or her choice until the class guesses who it is.

Fact or Fiction?

Give the class the name of a famous Jew from the past or present. The students are to brainstorm a list of everything they know about this person. Place the list on the board for everyone to see. Then have the students do some research about this person, making a list of the "real" facts they find as they do the research. Once their research is completed, have students compare their "facts" with the list they created before they did the research. Circle any item on the board that is incorrect. How did students do?

The Traveling Jew

Our ancestors have come from all over the world. If your curriculum includes the immigration of Jews to America, this activity is just right for you. Divide the class into small groups. Members are to talk among themselves and determine where some of their ancestors came from, then choose one country to use as a point of origin.

Each group is to thoroughly research that country, finding out as much as possible. Questions to consider include:

What was life for Jews like?
Where did Jews live?
What work did they engage in?
What foods did they eat?

What was the form of education?

What was the government like?

After students have finished their research, tell them to pretend they live in that country. However, they are going to have to move! They are all going to America. Give the "immigrants" paper to write on. Each person is to write two journal entries that describe (1) how he or she feels about leaving and (2) what he or she anticipates will be different in America.

Periodically remind students to write these journal entries as if they were the people involved with the move. Upon completion, they share their responses.

Life In . . .

. . . A shtetl, a kibbutz, the Lower East Side of New York, and so on. Turn your classroom into the location and period of time pertaining to your unit of study.

Divide the class into small groups of two or three and assign different aspects of Jewish life as they relate to your unit of study. Consider such areas as family life, religious life, education, culture, clothing, and work. As each group gathers the information, have students create posters, banners, newspapers, and the like to post around the room, eventually covering the wall space and perhaps even hanging things from the ceiling. Make the room come alive as a historical museum!

Then have groups prepare presentations based on their research. The presentations can be in the form of plays, musicals, television shows, newscasts, and so on. Students can even design costumes to wear that are reflective of the time period. Identify a date to invite parents for a special showing of what students have learned. Send written invitations—let the kids design one that reflects the period of time. The students will learn not only about a period of Jewish history, but how to solve problems cooperatively and to take pride in their efforts, thereby building up their self-esteem.

Flashback to the Past

Students can work individually or in small groups. Either let the students choose a period of time that interests them or assign a different period to each group or student. This activity may be spread out over several sessions.

Have students research the period, finding out as much as they can about Jews, Jewish life, and events during this period of time. To help students, either bring books and other relevant materials to class or arrange a visit to the synagogue library.

When their research is complete, students are to develop a story or poem that tells about the period. Encourage the students to be creative! Their work can become a song or ballad of the past, or students can use contemporary music to create a parody that tells the story. The contents of the story can be humorous, sad, tragic, blasé, questioning, autobiographical, or prophetic—the choice is up to the student or group. The main purpose, however, is to tell the story of the past. Have students set the scene using props and decorations—for example, posters, drawings, collages, banners, and period clothing—and allow students time to rehearse.

Set the date for their presentations. Students or groups can give their presentations at different times; just be sure you assign a date for each presentation. Or, you can make it a grand event and invite parents to join the festivities. *Note:* If this becomes a big to-do, send invitations to parents and place posters around the school so everyone is aware of when the event is going to take place.

Israel

Scramble the Skits for Israel

Divide the class into small groups. Give each group a topic to research about Israel. Some suggestions are religions and people, government, archaeological and tourist sites, agriculture, famous Israelis, and industry.

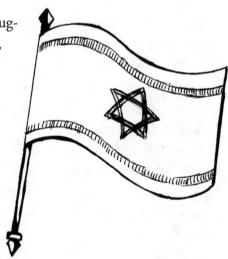

Once the groups have done their research, each group is to write and present a skit about its assigned topic. One catch, though! The group should include two or three obvious errors in the skit. The class then identifies the errors after each presentation, adding a fun dimension to the learning experience.

Jerusalem in the Bible

Divide the class into small groups. Give each group a list of five or six biblical quotes about Jerusalem. Each list should be different, but the quotes within a given list should share a common theme. For example, 2 Samuel 5:9, 1 Kings 2:10, and 1 Chronicles 15:1 all refer to Jerusalem as the "City of David." If necessary, look up "Jerusalem" in a Bible concordance.

Ask each group to identify the theme of the quotes and then to choose two or three. Once the group has selected the quotes, give each group a poster board, scratch paper, and markers. Have students create a poster that explains the different quotes they chose and illustrates what Jerusalem means to them. (Students should first sketch their ideas on the scratch paper.) Then they share their work with the class.

Role Playing

Divide the class into small groups. Ask each group to pretend it collectively is the prime minister of Israel. Give each group a different problem. Have members brainstorm solutions, then describe what they would do to solve the problem—and why!

Israel and Jerusalem in the *Siddur*

Divide the class into small groups. Give each group prayer books and a specific reading assignment (including page numbers), for example, *Birkat HaMazon* (Grace after the Meal), the weekday *Amidah,* or the Shabbat *Amidah.* Have group members identify the different statements they find in their assigned prayer referring to Israel or Jerusalem, writing down the statements as they find them. Students are also to write down the answers to guide questions that you provide. Include such questions as:

> What does this prayer say about Israel or Jerusalem?
> What does it say about the Jewish people?
> What are we praying for?

Students then share their responses and interpretations.

Israel's Geography

Either create an outline of the map of Israel or purchase blank outlines of the country. Inside, place stars at different locations you want the students to identify. Along the outside of the map, list specific sites of cities and outside of cities like Masada or Caesarea or the Sea of Galilee you would like the students to locate. For help, place a big map of Israel on the wall. If a student does not know where a site is located, he or she can look at the map to find its location. When they have finished, students will have learned a little of Israel's geography.

Alternative

Prepare several strips of paper naming sites in the State of Israel. Fold the strips and place them in a paper bag. Have available reference materials so students can research the different locations. Students choose partners; one of the pair then draws a slip of paper out of the bag. Using the materials you have provided, the pair is to learn about the chosen site and find it on the map. As students do their research, they are to make up index cards with important facts about the site. Upon completion of their research, they share their information with the class. As they make their presentation, they place a flag pin on a big map of the State of Israel, indicating the location of their site. The index cards can be placed to the side of the map, with string or narrow ribbons leading back to the location. You may want to use a different color for each site.

More Israel Geography

Place a large map of Israel up on the wall. Print on 3 x 5 index cards the names of a variety of places in Israel. Consider listing Hebrew names as well, in transliterated form if needed. Besides the cities, include rivers, seas, lakes, historical sites, and so forth. Place the index cards in a box and shake well. Students take turns pulling out an index card, reading the name of the site, and then locating it on the map. Have handy map pins and narrow ribbon or yarn in different colors. The student places a map pin on the location, pinning one end of the ribbon to the site, then brings the ribbon to the index card, pinning both along the side of the map. Continue until all the sites are located. You will end up with a maze of ribbons and map pins, and the students will have learned where a number of places are located in Israel.

State of Israel Quilt

This is a great project for the study of Israel. Let students create a quilt that tells all about the history of the State of Israel. First, talk to the students about what a quilt is. If possible, bring a hand-made quilt to class so they see what one looks like—some children may not have ever seen one. Tell children they are going to make a State of Israel quilt. What could they include in their quilt? What kind of pictures would tell the story of Israel? Do some brainstorming, making a list of all their suggestions. Possible list items include the flag, the state emblem, major agriculture and industrial products, geographical features, historical places, people, and events. Determine how big the quilt will be. Based on the planned size and the number of students in the class, you may want to let kids do more than one square. Or, get other classes—or even the whole school—involved in the project.

Prepare a paper quilt first, giving each student an exact-size paper square to use. Have each student (or class) choose a different theme. After doing some research, he or she draws a picture illustrating that theme and writes a caption to go with the picture. Once the student has finalized the design on paper, give him or her a fabric square to decorate. Students should use fabric markers or crayons. Be sure to follow the manufacturer's directions.

To complete the quilt, find one or two parents, or other congregation members, who would be willing to assemble the pieces and add the inside quilting material and the backing. Once it is finished, invite parents to view this very special quilt, then hang it prominently in the synagogue for all to see!

Israel's Chamber of Commerce

Divide the students into groups. Assign each group a city in Israel or let students choose one—just be sure there are no duplications. Tell students to pretend that their group works for the city's chamber of commerce. As some of its "employees," group members are to work together to write a letter providing information about the city: places of interest, climate, products produced in and around the city, historical and religious sites, and so forth. Have the groups share the completed letters.

A Visit to Israel

Post the names of different cities or locations in Israel around the room. To make it more exciting, add some pictures of the cities. Students choose a partner with whom to work. Assign each pair a location or let the students choose—just be sure there are no duplications. Prepare a list of questions to guide the students in their "travels." Your list could look something like this:

What is the city's population and ethnic makeup?
What is its geographic location in Israel?
What natural, agricultural, and industrial resources are nearby?
What religious sites are found in the city?
What historical sites are in the city or nearby?
What is the history of this place?

Now tell students to imagine that they are actually visiting the site—meeting people, eating with families, praying in synagogues, and so forth. As they do their research, children are to record their "experiences," describing what foods they ate, people they met, special times they had, and other highlights of the visit. Students then prepare a colorful presentation of their "travels."

Map of Israel Quiz Game

You will need a large map that depicts Israel as well as the neighboring countries. Place this on the wall. Prepare a number of quiz statements on index cards. Some examples are:

Israel signed a peace agreement with the country to the south.
It begins with the letter *H* and is the largest port in Israel.
David Ben-Gurion made his home here.
It begins with the letter *S* and was the home of Jewish mystics.

Prepare at least twelve cards, then let the students prepare at least twelve more. When you have twenty-four or more quiz statements, you are ready to play the game.

Divide the class into small groups. One member of the group draws a card, another reads the statement, and then the group confers on the answer. A group member gives the answer and identifies the location on the map. Each correct answer is worth a point. Continue playing until all the quiz statements have been used. If the group answers incorrectly, it loses its turn and the next group gets a chance to answer.

Edible Israel Scavenger Hunt

You will need M&M's or some other small candies, shoestring licorice, plastic bags, and a large map of Israel for each group.

Place maps of Israel on the floor for each group. Mark different sites with the M&M's—these will be the sites the students will want to visit.

Design your scavenger hunt so that students will be moving all over the map of Israel, discovering different locations. You will need at least fifteen to twenty sites for students to locate. The scavenger hunt clues could include some of the following:

Find Montefiore's Windmill. *[Jerusalem]*
The walls came tumbling down here. *[Jericho]*
Where the Dead Sea Scrolls were found. *[Qumran]*
Desert fortress built by Herod. *[Masada]*

Divide class into small groups. Give each group a bag containing shoestring licorice and a list of the hunt. Explain to the students that as they "travel" throughout Israel locating the different sites, they are to lay a "road" of shoestring licorice to show the path they have taken. Have some extra candy for children to snack on at journey's end. Want to make this a healthy trip? Use carrot strips and pretzel sticks or nuggets.

Seeking Peace in Israel

The Mideast peace process is a difficult one, as we all know. It may be hard for some, if not all of the students to fully understand what is taking place. To help them grasp what is happening, try comparing the situation to their own everyday lives.

Talk about disputes that may arise within a family. Either as a class or individually—and this will depend on how comfortable the kids feel with one another—do some brainstorming to come up with a list of the disputes that have occurred in their own families. Then discuss ways the disputes could be or have been settled peacefully. What are some of the peaceful methods students have used? What was easy to do? What was difficult?

Next, do the same for school. How are disputes there settled peacefully? Now it might be easier to take a look at the peace process taking place and understand the difficulties encountered by both sides. Relate their own experiences to the events occurring in Israel.

Israel's Neighbors

One of the areas often neglected when learning about Israel—probably because there is never enough time to cover everything—is the study of the surrounding Arab countries. Yet, this knowledge is important to the understanding of the history of the State of Israel. It is also key to understanding the whole peace process. Here are a few activities that could be done during the course of two or three class sessions.

Prepare in advance a basic planning sheet that lists all the information the students will need to find. Your planning sheet could look something like this:

53

Name of country: _____

Date established: _____

Relationship with Israel: _____

Capital: _____

Population: _____

Major bodies of water: _____

Type of land (desert, green areas, mountains, etc.): _____

Major economy (agriculture, industry, natural resources): _____

Special foods eaten: _____

Kind of clothing worn: _____

Religious or secular customs: _____

Other countries that border this one: _____

Divide the class into small groups. Assign one Arab country to each group. If the class is small enough try to use only those countries that actually border the State of Israel: Egypt, Jordan, Lebanon, and Syria. Otherwise feel free to use other countries in the region such as Saudi Arabia, Iraq, and Iran. Be sure the students can locate these countries on a map of the Middle East.

Pass out the planning sheets to each group and have students find the information requested. Have reference books available, or schedule a library visit. Upon completion of the research, ask each group to prepare a creative presentation of the information. For example, several Middle Eastern countries are famous for their rugs. A group might make a paper "Oriental rug," with the designs containing the information about the country. Just take a large brown paper bag, cut it open, and iron it smooth with a warm iron. Or, use butcher paper. Show the kids some pictures of Oriental rugs to give some layout ideas. Students could use crayons or markers to draw a fancy design for the border of their rug. They can use 4 x 6 index cards, or construction paper cut to size, to write the information on, then glue the cards to the paper rug. Draw fancy designs around each card to set it off. Students will also need to incorporate the country's name into the design. Finally, cut some "fringes" out of construction paper and glue them to the back of the rug. After all the groups have finished their presentations, hang the rugs on the wall.

History of Israel's Neighbors

I know it is sometimes difficult for our students to look at the past. However, there is much to be learned from it, especially with respect to the Mideast peace process. Much of what is taking place could be better understood if we knew of the past. Keep it simple. Divide the class into small groups, assign each group one country to study, and at the end of their research, each group will share what it learned.

Prepare a list of questions that students can use to take a step back in time. Your questions could look something like this:

Has the country had other names in the past?
Is so, what are they?
When did the country's name change and why?
What bodies of water still have the same names as they did in the past?
What was the relationship between these ancient countries and what is now the State of Israel?

To encourage them to be on the lookout for the answers to your questions, have the kids create a bulletin board titled "A Step Back in Time." You might even prepare a drawing of shoes or sandals with space for the students to write their information. Make a number of them and place them in an envelope attached to the bulletin board. Tell the students that as they research their projects, if they come across an interesting tidbit of information from the past they can take one of the sandals and write the information down, then put it on the bulletin board. Before you know it, your class will have created an extensive bulletin board on Israel and her neighbors' past.

Building Jerusalem

Gather together pictures of the city of Jerusalem. Make enlarged copies and distribute them to the students. Also give students pale yellow paper (to simulate the look of Jerusalem stone) and pencils. Tell children to look at the different shapes of the buildings. How different are they from buildings in America? Ask students to try drawing outlines of some of the buildings, making their collection as diverse as possible. They can draw synagogues, apartment buildings, museums, even the wall around the Old City. Allow students to make as many drawings as they'd like, sketching light lines on each building to simulate large blocks of stone. Then, cut out the shapes and laminate. Make stands by cutting strips out of card stock and bending them so that when they are glued to the "building," it will stand up. Glue the stands to the back of each building. Let the students arrange their city of Jerusalem on a table, patterning the layout after the pictures the class has been viewing.

A Spider Web of Israel's History

Cover your bulletin board with brown paper. Tell the students they are going to create a giant "spider web" of an event or person in Israel's history. First arrange white yarn all over the board to resemble a spider web. Cut out and have ready a number of different-size oval black spider bodies. Have the students identify the main subject of your unit of study. Say, for example, that you are covering the creation of the State of Israel, with emphasis on the role of David Ben-Gurion. Prepare the board by writing Ben-Gurion's name on a large spider body and placing it in the center of the web. Do some brainstorming with the students and make a list of at least eight character traits of Ben-Gurion. Children write these traits on smaller black ovals, placing them evenly on each side of the central spider body. Attach the ovals to the body with pieces of black pipe cleaner or yarn. As they study the creation of the State of Israel, students can add other names and events that are involved with the creation of the State. Place the names on smaller black oval bodies. For people, include the character traits of each individual. By the end of your unit of study, you will have a history web of the State of Israel. This activity can be used for other events or people in Jewish history.

Jewish Values, Concepts, and Symbols

THE SYNAGOGUE

Years ago, when I was youth group adviser, I attended an adviser's workshop. One statement made by Rabbi Hank Skirball has remained in my mind all these years because I thought it was so important. He said that our role is to make the synagogue a second home for the youth—a place where they feel safe and happy to be. We need to make it a place where they *want* to be! So here are three activities you can use to help kids realize how special their synagogue is.

Synagogue Walk 1

Take the class on a walk through the synagogue. Be sure each child has a pen and paper for taking notes. Look at the bulletin boards, and at any historic exhibits that might be in glass cabinets; visit the library, other classrooms, the kitchen, and the rabbi's office and study; spend time in the sanctuary really investigating what's there and even just looking out the windows. While you visit these locations, ask the kids such questions as: What do you see that you like? What is there about this place that makes it special? What is there about the synagogue that you are proud of? What is there about the synagogue that makes you feel you belong here? What would you like to change? What do you want to stay the same? What else would you like to see in the synagogue? As the students think about these questions, give them time to write some notes in response. When you have completed your walk, go back to your classroom and discuss with the whole class what students like best about the synagogue. Pass out drawing paper and have each student draw a picture of what he or she considers his or her special place in the synagogue. Have students add captions describing the drawings. Combine all the pictures into a class book.

Synagogue Walk 2

Tell the children you are going to take them on a tour of the synagogue. Talk with them about what they might see on this tour. Make notes of what they describe. As you take them on the tour, point out the things they see, yet didn't mention. Back in the classroom, have the children describe the synagogue and what they saw. Write each child's response on a colorful strip of paper.

Place on the wall or floor a large piece of white butcher paper. Work with the children to help them draw a mural of the synagogue, including everything they saw on their tour. Help them place the paper strip descriptions in the appropriate area of their mural. When complete, hang the mural in the hall for everyone to see.

Synagogue Scavenger Hunt

Develop a set of clues about places of importance in the synagogue. Include as well references to those people who are essential to the operation of the synagogue on a daily basis. Have one or two clues for each place and person. Copy the list and divide the class into small groups. Give each group a copy of the clues. Instruct the students they are to identify locations and people. When they have identified a person, they are to have him or her sign under the clue. Give children a specific time when they are to return to the classroom, whether they have completed the scavenger hunt or not. When they have returned, have the groups share their experiences as they did their hunt, telling what they learned about their synagogue. *Note:* Prior to the day of the hunt, be sure the staff of the synagogue are aware of what your class is going to be doing so they can be prepared for the interruptions.

OTHER VALUES AND CONCEPTS

What Makes a Beautiful Day?

Everyone will have a different interpretation of this question—that's okay. A lot of what students consider special can be seen as "God created" or "God inspired."

Talk with the students about what they might consider to be a beautiful day. It could be as simple as walking on the beach, sitting in the sunshine, or smelling the roses (something we should always make time for!). It could be spending time with friends doing what they all like best: going to the mall, watching movies, and so on. Do some brainstorming with students and remind them to be accepting of all suggestions.

After the brainstorming, ask each student to draw a picture that represents what he or she considers to be a "Special Day." Encourage those students who say they can't draw to just use their imaginations, reminding them that we are not looking for great works of art. Tell the students that they alone will interpret the drawings and are the only ones who need to understand them—so students are to draw to their heart's content what represents, to them, a beautiful day. When all have completed this task, each student shares his or her drawing, explaining as necessary. Let each identify which activities were God created and which were God inspired.

Ecology in the Bible

Either copy the following Torah portions from the Bible, or have students use their own Bibles to read these portions: Leviticus 19:23–25; Leviticus 25:2–7; Deuteronomy 8:1 and 7–10; and Deuteronomy 20:19–20.

Divide the class into small groups. Tell them to read the material and make two lists that describe (1) the land the Israelites are about to enter and (2) what the Israelites were to do to protect the land and the trees.

Have groups share their lists, making one composite list. With the students, talk about the benefits that the Israelites would derive from the land and the trees. Using the commandments in the Torah, discuss lessons we can describe that can help us take better care of our environment.

Pathways Through Jewish Life

This takes a little preparation, but it will be worth the effort. Prepare a sheet with a list of mitzvot from the Torah. Here are just a few examples:

Do not give false testimony. (Exodus 20:13)

Do not treat another person unfairly. (Leviticus 19:16)

You shall not hate your fellow person in your heart. (Leviticus 19:17)

Do not break your word. (Numbers 30:3)

Do not crave anything that is your neighbor's. (Deuteronomy 5:18)

Help those who are needy among you. (Deuteronomy 15:7)

Another source for a listing of mitzvot can be found in the *Encyclopedia Judaica*. Remember, there are 613 mitzvot, but you will only need to include around twenty-five or thirty on your list. Place your choices on a sheet of paper with the following instructions to the students:

> Judaism provides us with a road map. It's called Halachah, from the word *halach*, which means "walk." From this list of mitzvot, choose those that fit into your Jewish life.

Give the students time to review the list and make their choices. When they select a mitzvah, they are also to think about the reason for making it part of their life. When they have completed the list, ask each student to share some of his or her choices. How did the student arrive at each choice, and for what reasons?

Deeds of Loving-kindness

Have on hand a bunch of magazines and newspapers for the children to use. Prepare on colored 9 x 12 poster boards words that describe "deeds of loving-kindness." Your list of words can look something like this:

Chesed—Loving-kindness

Rachamim—Compassion

Ahavah—Love

Tzedakah—Righteousness (helping others accomplish their goals)

Tzaar Baalei Chayim—Caring for all living creatures

Place the posters around the room. Talk about these words with the children until they understand the meanings. Then let the children go through the magazines and newspapers to find pictures that relate to any of these words. Students can make a scrapbook of their pictures, printing the words next to the appropriate picture.

Alternative

You can also relate this to TV shows students watch. Ask them to identify any deeds of loving-kindness they observe on a show as they watch TV. The students keep a record of those shows demonstrating a relationship to any of these Jewish values. Students then bring their notes to the next class and share their findings.

G'milut Chasadim

Brainstorm with the kids about what they consider to be "good deeds." If necessary, guide them to realize that a good deed can be a simple action: writing a nice note to a new student, emptying the wastebasket, taking out the garbage without being told, setting the table with a smile, washing and drying the dishes or loading the dishwasher, washing the car, taking care of the family pet, or helping someone across the street. Once their list is completed, ask the students to copy it into a notebook or a journal. Give the students a time limit—say, two weeks—during which they should keep track of their good deeds. As he or she performs an act of loving-kindness the student should check it off the list. When time is up, ask volunteers to talk about how it felt to do all those good deeds. Who knows—you might have encouraged some of the students to get in the habit of helping others!

Bikur Cholim

There are many ways to fulfill the mitzvah of visiting the sick. This activity is one hospitalized children can appreciate long after they've gone home.

Select a picture book that is no longer used in the classroom but is still in good condition. (Or, ask children to donate a used book from home.) You will need a tape recorder and a means of signaling when to turn the page. Some possibilities are ringing a bell, banging a drum, tapping a spoon on a glass, or blowing a kazoo. Ask a student to read the story slowly, clearly, and with feeling—that is, speaking with a lot of expression to make the story interesting and exciting. After the student has practiced reading the story, he or she finds a quiet place and records the story. Another student signals when it is time to turn the page. Upon completion of the taping, wrap the book and the tape as a gift for a child in the hospital. (You may want to find some parental volunteers to go with their children to the hospital and deliver the presents personally.)

Hiddur P'nei Zakein

The mitzvah of honoring the elderly can be fulfilled in many ways. The activity suggested here is a great way for the children to gain a better understanding and acceptance of elderly people. Contact the director of a local residence home and tell him or her that you would like to create a senior pen pals program with your students and residence members. Usually the director is happy to match up students with residents who are willing to participate. Soon the letters will be flying back and forth. The students can make and send holiday cards to their pen pal or ask his or her opinion on questions that trouble them. Students and pen pals can even share their experiences in school, discussing the differences and similarities.

Honesty is the Best Policy

The kids might think that honesty is a secular value, but references to the importance of being honest are quite prevalent in Jewish text. So, take some time and make them aware of this true Jewish value!

Ask students to explain what honesty means to them. Compare students' definition of "honesty" with the definition in the dictionary. What are the similarities and differences?

Next, divide the class into small groups. Give each group a different situation that requires some form of being honest, for example:

Finding a wallet full of money in a movie theater.
Keeping a secret after promising not to gossip or share it.
Admitting to making a mistake and not blaming someone else.
Receiving too much change from a cashier.
Telling a friend the truth rather than what he or she wants to hear.
Explaining the real reason you didn't turn in your homework instead of using "the dog ate it" as an excuse.

Compile and copy verses from various Jewish sources, such as the following:

Keep far from a false charge. (Exodus 23:7)
You must not carry false rumors; . . . you shall not give perverse testimony in a dispute so as to be in favor of the mighty. (Exodus 23:1–2)
When you sell property to your neighbor, or buy any from your neighbor, you shall not wrong one another. (Leviticus 25:14)
Truth springs out of the earth. (Psalm 85:12)
Happy are those whose way is blameless. (Psalm 119:1)

These are just a few examples. Tell each group it has ten minutes to create a short three-minute skit demonstrating what members would do in the particular situation in light of what Judaism says about honesty. Each group then presents its dramatic skit. After each skit, talk about the group's response to the situation. Was the solution an honest one? Let students come up with different ways to handle the situation in an honest manner.

After students have finished their skits and discussed them, talk with students about what Judaism says about being honest. Being honest is very much a part of Jewish life; knowing this, what impact does being honest have on students? Talk about it.

One more thing to discuss. Ask the students to think about ways their actions might affect others when confronted with situations that require honesty. What happens when they tell a lie and the wrong person is punished? Will dishonesty solve a problem, or just delay it and maybe even make it worse?

Show Me the Money!

Jews have always been known for taking care of their own. This dates back to biblical times: we are told in Leviticus 19:9 to leave a corner of the field for the widow and the orphan. Over the years, many Jewish organizations have been created to assist the Jewish people with their varying needs. *The American Jewish Year Book,* published annually by the American Jewish Committee, has an extensive list of such organizations. Another source is the Ziv Tzedakah Fund, Inc. To request a brochure, write to 384 Wyoming Ave., Millburn, NJ 07041, or visit Ziv's website at **www.ziv.org.** Their list includes some excellent organizations that are not as well known. **www.just-tzedakah.org** is also a good source.

Divide the class into small groups. Assign each group a specific focus: the elderly, the poor, widows, orphans, hunger, culture, education, and so on. Each group is to identify those organizations that provide support for their specific area. Then, students are to research these organizations and find out what each organization does, how it provides support to those it aids, and how it raises its funds.

Upon completion of the research, each group is to prepare a large poster depicting the need it focused on and the different organizations that address this need. Encourage each group to choose *one* organization with which members are most impressed and that they think does the best job. What makes this organization effective? Each group shares its findings with the class and tells what criteria it used in deciding the best organization.

For closure, have the class choose one or two organizations it wishes to support and organize a fund-raising effort involving the whole school, if possible. Or, donate your class's *tzedakah* funds to these organizations.

Jewish Values and the Holidays

When teaching the different holidays, we often forget the Jewish values inherent in each one. These values are as important as the holiday itself. Here is an example of what you could do for Shabbat:

Prepare a sheet that lists at least ten Jewish values. Your list could look something like this:

Study of Torah
Covenant
Oneg Shabbat
G'milut chasadim
Tzedakah
Respect for parents
Loving your neighbor as yourself
Visiting the sick
Truth
Feeding the hungry

Ask the students to rank-order the list, with number 1 being the most important and number 10 being the least important. Upon completion, do some sharing by those who wish. Put these aside.

Alternative Values List

Divide the class into small groups. Give each group some prayer books. Students are to go through the prayer books and find as many Jewish values as they can during a specific time limit, say, ten minutes. List their selections on the board. Let the students choose together the ten Jewish values they consider the most important. Then, individually, each student is to rank-order them as above. Students share their responses.

Then, take the two Shabbat commandments, Exodus 20:8–11 and Deuteronomy 5:12–15, and place them side by side on a sheet of paper. Leave room for the students to compile a list of Jewish values. Copy and give one to each student.

On a separate paper ask the students to compare the two and make a list of all the differences and similarities they can identify. Have students then list all of the Jewish values they can identify in the two commandments.

For Your Information

The Shabbat commandments emphasize the following Jewish values:

1. All people are created equal and should be treated equally.
2. The poor, the humble, the stranger, and the slave are equals.
3. All social differences are annulled.
4. We are to show care and concern for all living creatures.
5. Shabbat unites Jews around the world *(K'lal Yisrael)*.
6. We are made in God's image and we have the power to be creative.
7. We should be aware of and care for our environment.

See how many of these the students can identify. When they have completed their listings, have them share their responses. Have students compare their Jewish values with their rank-order list. What values are the same? What are different? Would students change their lists?

Quotes About Jewish Values and Concepts

There are numerous Jewish quotes stating a Jewish value or concept. Some sample quotes are as follows:

"Let us walk in the Light of the Lord." (Isaiah 2:5)
"Judge not your neighbor until you have been in his place." (Hillel, *Pirkei Avot* 2:4)
"Seek good, not evil, that you may live." (Amos 5:14)

There are many books of quotations that you can search for more ideas, as well as many Internet websites. You can make use of these quotes in a number of ways:

1. Make posters of a good number of quotes and place them around the room so the students can become familiar with them. Be sure to include where the quote came from and who said it. Periodically change the posters or move them around.
2. Make a list of quotes you would like to use throughout the year. Periodically place one on a large, colorful strip of paper so everyone can see it. Ask students to read the quote. Do some brainstorming to determine what it means, what it is saying to us, and how we can apply it to our lives.

3. Prepare a list of one-line quotes that are related to your unit of study. At the beginning of each class session, hand out copies of the quote on a notebook-size sheet of paper. Depending on the students, they can do any (or all) of the following:

> Restate the quote in their own words.
> Draw a picture that expresses its meaning.
> Write a short paragraph stating what the quote means to them.
> Identify the person who said it.
> Write a short paragraph about the person who said it.

Give each student a folder or binder to place the sheets in. By the end of the year, students will have compiled a book of quotations of Jewish values and concepts.

Wall of Jewish Values

This could be a year-long project for any age group. Set aside one wall of the classroom for this activity, or find a specific space where a "wall" can be constructed. Place a title at the top. Prepare pieces of card stock to be used as "building blocks" for the wall. Any color can be used, just be creative, especially if you want to call attention to your wall. Place these "blocks" in the designated space. You should also have handy tacky adhesive and markers.

As you go through your unit of study, have students identify the Jewish value found within a given lesson. Discuss it with students to be sure they understand what it means and how it can be applied in today's world. The student, or students, who have identified the Jewish value for the day can put it on the building block and attach it to the wall. Be sure the blocks are spaced so they take on the appearance of a brick wall. By the end of the year you should have completed a class "Wall of Jewish Values."

"Krazy for Kosher"

Not all Jews keep kosher, but many do chose to. A number of years ago, an article with this title appeared in the *Detroit Jewish News*. Apparently, more Americans than ever are interested in purchasing kosher food, regardless of their religion. They see the health benefits in the stringent inspection standards dictated by kosher law. For example, for a cow to be certified kosher, it has to be healthy to begin with. If there are any signs of disease or flaws, the whole animal is discarded. Kosher standards differ from the food-safety regulations of the federal government. People generally believe if food, especially meat, is kosher, it's of better quality.

Given the renewed interest in keeping kosher, why not plan a lesson where the children learn about another part of our Jewish heritage? Divide the class into small groups. Give each group an assignment to investigate such items as the following:

The laws of *kashrut* (keeping kosher)
The symbols of kosher food
Forbidden foods
Reasons for keeping kosher according to tradition
Benefits of keeping kosher for health purposes

Plan a trip to the library so children can do some research. Or provide them with the necessary information. There are also a number of sites on the Internet that address the laws of *kashrut*. Once each group has completed its research, members are to prepare a report sharing their information with the entire class. The report can be in any form of media they choose.

Then, ask the students to take an inventory of the foods at home, making a list of the kosher foods that their family uses. Students will be surprised at how many items have kosher symbols on them. Also, ask parents to take their child grocery shopping, preferably before the next class. The child is to bring a notebook and pencil and list all the kosher foods found throughout the store, not just in the kosher foods section. The next class session, students share their findings with the class. This can also be a fun in-class activity. You can bring in different foods with a variety of kosher symbols on them and have the students learn through eating the food in class.

Spirituality

This activity is based on an article written by Rabbi Jeffrey Salkin, "How to Be a Truly Spiritual Jew." If you want to read the entire article, it appeared in the Fall 1995 issue of *Reform Judaism*. It also can be found on the website of Synagogue 2000. Just go to **www.syn2000.org/Learning/readings.html**, then scroll down until you find the article.

The words "spiritual" and "spirituality" have been religious buzzwords for a number of years now. I myself cringe every time I hear them because I wonder if people really know what they mean when they say something like: "I'm looking for a spiritual experience." As a result, I have designed this activity to

Spirituality Is About *Kedushah*: Holiness

"But all the children of Israel had light in their dwellings." Each one of us possesses a holy spark, but not everyone exhibits it to the best advantage. It is like the diamond that cannot cast its luster if buried in the earth. When disclosed in its appropriate setting, there is light, as from a diamond, in each one of us.

• • •

Israel Baal Shem Tov, who founded Chasidism in the eighteenth century and was also known as the Besht, once said:

The Torah commands us "Fire shall be kept burning upon the altar continually, it shall not go out" (Leviticus 6:6). Our heart is the altar. In every occupation, let the spark of the holy fire remain within you, so that you may fan it into a flame.

• • •

Rabbi Jeffrey Salkin (*Reform Judaism,* Fall 1995) wrote:

Spirituality is about *kedushah,* Holiness. *Kedushah* is an attitude towards life. "Holiness" means to venerate the Divine, to seek out the mystery of God, to sense that some realms are set apart, unique, linking heaven and earth, and manifesting a shared reality with the Divine. Holiness is where "spirituality" becomes "Judaism." Through disciplined participation in authentic Jewish acts that increase our sense of holiness, we connect ourselves to our people, to our history, to God, and to that ill-defined thing called spirituality.

In looking at your outline, consider where you would find "Holiness and the Sparks of the Divine."

> The head: the seat of mental thoughts and deeds
> The heart: the seat of emotional deeds
> The torso: the seat of physical actions and deeds

You are to place, within your body outline, answers to the following questions:

> What acts increase your sense of holiness?
> What acts of holiness bring you closer to God?
> What are the right behaviors for holiness?
> What are your obligations? To others, to yourself?
> What do you owe the world? your community? your family?
> How do you let God in?
> What can you do to fan the spark of the Divine into a flame?

help students, both young and old, to better understand the meaning of "spirituality."

You will need:

Newsprint, a chalkboard, or a flip chart
6-foot piece of butcher paper, one per group
Felt-tip markers, one per person
Copy of the handout for each person (on pages 67–68)

Part I

With the whole class, do some brainstorming to define the word "spirituality" without looking in the dictionary. Write students' responses down on one side of the blackboard. Upon completion of the brainstorming, move on to the next part of the activity, but leave the brainstorming list on the board.

Part II

Next, divide the class into small groups of three or four. Give each group one sheet of butcher paper, plus a felt-tip marker for each person in the group. Tell students to place the paper on the floor. One person is to lie down on the butcher paper while another member of the group draws an outline of the person.

Pass out the handout and together read the midrashim and the quote from Rabbi Salkin. Go over the portion of the handout that discusses the different parts of the body, explaining what they could mean. Tell students they are to answer the questions on the sheet, placing short, one- or two-word responses in the appropriate place on the body outline. Give the students time to discuss the answers within the group. This may take about forty-five minutes. When students have completed this part of the activity, ask each group to share its responses, then hang the body outline on the wall. After each group has shared, go back to the original brainstorming list of students' definitions of "spirituality." How would they define "spirituality" now? Place their new list next to the first one. You should find that the second list is different from the first, reflecting students' realization that spirituality comes from within.

Prayer

AN ENCOUNTER WITH PRAYER

There has been much discussion about how we teach prayer to our students. Some teach the prayers by rote, that is, memorization. Others say that with this method, the prayers have no meaning to the kids. I am inclined to agree. Over the years I have heard comments from the kids about how the words have no meaning; we keep repeating the same thing every time, there  is no rhyme or reason to the prayers, and so on. As a result of these comments, I have put together a program that is specifically designed to help the students understand what they are saying.

I find that most young people have difficulty praying in the formal sense. Yet there are times when a person might have a truly "religious" (read: "spiritual") experience in which he or she has the sense of being close to God. We cannot teach students how to experience this feeling. However, we *can* help them confront some of their inner conflicts about the worship experience. You will need to remind the kids that we pray with words, initially because that was all we knew, although, today we also pray with music and dance if we are so moved. Remind students that words can be soothing, annoying, or uplifting, depending on how they are used.

The following activities are designed to help the students deal with some of the questions about meaningful prayer.

SPECIFIC PRAYERS

Yotzer Or/Maariv Aravim

These two prayers follow the *Bar'chu*. They acknowledge God's role in Creation. *Yotzer Or* is used in the morning service, and *Maariv Aravim* in the evening service.
You will need:

Prayerbook or copy of prayer for each student
Roll of white adding-machine tape, cut into three-foot sections, with several sections for each pair of students
Fine-line markers or colored pencils

String or ribbon
Clothespins or paper clips

Read one of the prayers together, then discuss with the students what they consider are some of the "wonders of God." You could even give some examples of your own. Do this for a few minutes, until you are sure they understand that not all of God's wonders are large in scale; rather, some are quite small in style.

Students then choose partners and do some brainstorming of their own to make a list of God's wonders of Creation. After a few minutes, ask each pair to share its list. Students should feel free to add any of the other students' ideas to their own list. Now, give each pair several sections of the adding-machine tape and some markers or colored pencils, telling them they are to create banners illustrating at least ten of God's wonders of Creation that really impress them. Upon completion, hang their "Wonders of God" banners on the string or ribbon you have placed on the wall around the room. Use the clothespins or paper clips for easy hanging.

Alternative

Ask the children to keep a journal of magical moments in nature when they have seen or experienced something special. Encourage students to take time to look around and to be aware! Give them some examples: the first bud of spring, the first robin, a rainbow, a colorful sunset. Tell students to remember the wonderful moment that took place by writing as much detail as possible about what they have seen or experienced.

After a specific time—say, a few weeks—ask the students to share the wonders they have seen. After sharing, look at *Yotzer Or/Maariv Aravim* prayers. Do some brainstorming with the students, making a list of everything in our natural world for which they praise God. Compare their list to the different miracles or wonders students have seen.

The *Sh'ma* and its Blessings

Here is an activity that might help the students better understand this prayer. Read the *Sh'ma* and *V'ahavta* in Hebrew (or transliteration if necessary) and in English. Then prepare the following handout for the students:

> **You shall love the Lord your God with all your mind, with all your strength, with all your being.**
>
> The path to the love of God is through the love of others; I do not love God until I love my neighbor as myself.

71

Set these words, which I command you this day, upon your heart.

> Jewish faith unites mind and heart. Even as my mind seeks to understand life's meaning, so may my life show love for all created things.

Teach them faithfully to your children; speak of them in your home and on your way, when you lie down and when you rise up.

> We do not teach our children by words alone. May I make my life and actions into good teachings, for in my conduct I must exemplify Torah.

Bind them as a sign upon your hand; let them be a symbol before your eyes; inscribe them on the doorposts of your house, and on your gates.

> Let my home glow with the beauty of our heritage. Let my doors be opened wide to wisdom and to righteousness.

Be mindful of all My mitzvot and do them; so shall you consecrate yourselves to your God.

> Each mitzvah is a way to holiness. The mitzvot elevate our humanity. Let me learn to use them to magnify the Divine in myself and in the world.

After reading, ask the students to think for a few minutes about what they just read. Then, divide the class into small groups. Ask each group to make a list of all the ways in which God shows love for Israel and all human beings. Allow a few minutes, then ask them to set this list aside.

Next, hand out a copy of the following to each student:

Reb Nachman of Bratzlav said: "Humans reach in three directions. We reach up to God, out to other people, and into our own heart. The secret is that all three directions are really the same. When we reach out to another person, we find ourselves and God; when we find God, we find others and the real us. When I find myself, I reach God and other people."

Ask students to read this quote and then, in their same groups, make a list of ways in which an individual reaches and shows love for another. After they complete their lists, have students share and compare the new lists with the previous ones. What are the similarities and differences?

Close the activity by having each student complete the following sentence with the first words that come to mind:

I can show my love for God and other human beings by ————.

Music Can Make the World Go Around!

Obtain a tape or compact disc of Debbie Friedman's "And You Shall Love." Give each student a white piece of drawing paper that is then folded into six sections. Have crayons or markers available for each student, as well as prayer books or copies of the prayer.

Read the *V'ahavta* prayer first and then play the song, asking the students to listen carefully to the words and what the prayer is saying. Then play the song again and ask the students to draw six pictures, one in each square of the folded paper, representing six of the major concepts that this prayer is telling us to do.

A Visual Look at Prayer

Not all prayers will lend themselves to this activity, but the *V'ahavta* and *Maariv Aravim* certainly do. Distribute to students copies of a prayer in Hebrew and English. Have them read the prayer and underline the words and phrases they think are the most important. Invite students to share with the class their choices and the reasons for them.

Then, divide the class into small groups. Ask each group to design a pictograph of the prayer, using pictures and symbols, but with as few letters and words as possible. Keep in mind that the results will be the group's interpretation of the prayer. It may help members to find meaning that might not have been there for them before. Share the results of their creativity and encourage discussion.

Jewish Geography

Where Do All the Jewish People Live?

There are Jewish communities all over the world. Some are large, most are small, but they *are* there.

For the opening lesson, begin with a "going-away party." Decorate the room with balloons, streamers, and travel posters, and place a "Jewish passport" on each student's desk. Have a big map of the world, if possible, as your bulletin board. Explain to the students they are going to be visiting different Jewish communities around the world. Divide the class into small groups. Have each group choose or assign it a different country to investigate. Depending on how broad the unit is, you may wish to choose countries from the same or different continents.

Schedule a visit to the library for students to research some of the major cities and to identify where Jewish communities are located. The Internet is a good resource, of course. An excellent book is *The Jewish Traveler*, edited by Alan M. Tigay. But the *Encyclopedia Judaica* will also be a good source. Many of the cities have either a Jewish community center, or a person identified as the leader of the community. The students can write these people for additional information. Once students have identified cities with Jewish communities, have students make a list of all these cities. Within each group, the students need to divide the cities among them and find out as much as they can about the Jewish community in each city.

Tell the students they are going to create a magazine to be placed in the synagogue library. This way, the information they gather will be available to anyone traveling to any of the locations. As students do their research, they should consider how they will present the information they are gathering in an attractive, informative manner.

After students have finished their research, invite them to identify the different locations on your world map. You can use colorful map pins or markers to pinpoint the spots. Attach thin, colorful ribbons or string to index cards on the side of the map that give a one- or two-line description of each location.

When the students have gathered and organized all their information, they should decide how best to arrange their travel magazine: by country, city, alphabetical order, and so on. Design a cover, a page to tell who was involved, a resource list, and the like. Then give students time to write, draw, and prepare their materials for the travel magazine.

Jewish Geography Activity Squares

Prepare a chart with sixteen squares to hand out to each student. In each square, place an activity that the students are to complete on a separate sheet. When they have completed the activity, they can color in the square or place an X through it.

Let's say the class is studying Jews around the world. You can give each student, or group of students, a different site in the world to visit. The activities they have to do could look something like this:

List three things you want to see when you visit this place.
Draw a flag to represent your location.
For each letter in the name of your location, write the name of a person, place, or thing found there.
Create a bumper sticker to advertise your location.
Draw a picture of one thing that can be purchased only in your location.
Create a map of your location identifying places to see.
Develop a booklet that shows the flora and fauna of your location.
List three things you would take with you on your visit.
Write a menu for a meal, using foods that are found in this location.
Describe briefly the Jewish worship service you attended.
Draw a picture of how Jews in this location celebrate Shabbat.
List three reasons why you would want to live in this location.
Describe how the Jews make a living in this location.
Write a short story describing what Jewish teens there do for fun.
Write about the highlights of your visit.
Describe how you would encourage others to visit this Jewish community.

Give the students time to gather information about their location. When they have completed the chart, they share their findings with the entire class.

Historical Travel Agents

Divide the class into small groups. Provide a list of different locations where Jews have settled over the years. Let each group choose a location, or assign a different one to each group.

Groups are to research the locations to determine what life was like for the Jews there. Students are to look at the government, climate, and natural resources, as well as what the location had to offer the Jews. After gathering all the information, each group is to design a travel brochure that contains the information members have discovered. Remind them that a travel brochure is used to sell a location to would-be tourists. Students will need to make the brochure attractive so others will want to pay them a visit. Upon completion each group shares its travel brochures with the class.

A Potpourri of Ideas

These ideas can be used for just about any subject matter.

Fact or Fiction

This is most effective when used with a research or reading assignment. Divide the class into small groups. Give each group a different reading or research assignment.

Tell the groups that as they do their research or reading they are to create a "Fact or Fiction" book. Each page of the book is to have a statement and an illustration on the front. On the back, the students tell whether the statement is fact or fiction, explaining the truth of the matter and providing any additional important information.

Upon completion, each group designs a cover and arranges the pages in the proper order. The group then shares its book with the class, seeing if the students can identify fact from fiction.

A Book of Riddles

Either individually, or in pairs, students choose a famous Jewish person or event, in the Bible or Jewish history. Be sure each choice is different. Give the students time to do some research about the subject. Students then develop a set of who, what, where, and when clues about it, keeping everything short and simple.

Give each student or pair a 9 x 12 piece of construction paper, four library pockets, four index cards to put into the library pockets, and glue. Students write either Who?, What?, Where?, or When? on each library pocket then glue the four pockets onto the construction paper. Children give their paper a heading that can also be a clue to their person or event. On one side of each index card, they write Who? What? Where? or When? On the back of the card they write the corresponding clue to the question. They place the cards into the appropriate pocket. For example: the clues for David Ben-Gurion might be:

Who: First prime minister of Israel
What: Fought to establish the State of Israel
Where: Born in Poland but later moved to what was then Palestine
When: Declared Israel to be a state in 1948

Compile all the riddles in one booklet for everyone to enjoy.

Top Secret Mystery Stories

Based on your unit of study, give each child a slip of paper with a different secret topic. Tell students not to share this with anyone! Each student is to find some private space to write and illustrate a short story based on his or her secret topic. Children then share their completed stories with the whole class.

Human Tic-tac-toe

You have heard of musical chairs—well, how about human tic-tac-toe? You will need nine chairs, placed in three rows of three each. Divide your class into two teams. Begin the game by asking the first person in one team a review question. If it is answered correctly, the team decides which chair that student is to occupy. If the question is answered incorrectly, the student goes to the end of the line, and the opposing team has a chance to respond to the same question. Once a student sits down in a chair he or she cannot change seats. The game ends when a team gets tic-tac-toe. Play as often as needed to complete your review.

Learning Walls

With the students, gather together from old books, workbooks, magazines, newspapers, and so on, articles and pictures pertaining to your unit of study. Students' families can participate as well by sending articles and pictures from home. Students group the materials together in appropriate sections. For example, for a unit on "Famous Jewish Women," students might collect materials on Henrietta Szold, Golda Meir, and Ruth Bader Ginsburg. Once you have enough materials to get your Learning Wall started, plan out displays of the gathered materials. Students attach them to the walls of the classroom in an attractive manner. Students will be responsible for setting up the Learning Wall and maintaining the wall displays.

Throughout the year, the students may add additional materials to the wall: work children have done in class, other information they have found, descriptions of books they have discovered on the subject matter, and their own creative materials. All these get attached to the wall in the appropriate section. A few times during the school year, have a scavenger hunt (a good means for review). Work with students to create questions for the hunt; making sure that the answers can be found on the Learning Wall. To encourage cooperation, allow the students to help one another or even to work in pairs or small groups.

With this kind of ongoing project, there is always something to do in the classroom. Plus, it makes a wonderful display for parents when they come to visit.

A Large Mosaic

As a closure for a unit of study or even a special event taking place, your class could make a "mosaic" based on your unit of study. You will need 2-inch-square pieces of white tag board (several per student), plus scraps of paper the same size as the tag board; markers, white glue, and a large poster board. Give each student a blank "tile"—or piece of white tag board—on which is to be drawn a picture or design representative of the unit. Give them some scratch paper to practice on first until they are satisfied with the design.

Students can create as many tiles as they desire—even a series of them to tell a story. Glue the finished tiles onto a large poster board, fitting the tiles together to make a mosaic. Hang it on the wall or place outside your classroom so others can see their work of art.

Proper Order

Write a short story based on your unit of study. Type the story into the computer, but leave two or three spaces between the lines. Print and copy enough for each pair of children in the class. Keep one copy in its complete form as an answer key. Mount the story on tag board and laminate or cover with clear contact paper. Cut into sentence strips. Place each set of strips in an envelope and distribute to the pairs of students. Tell students they are to place the strips in a logical story sequence. Upon completion, compare each pair's sequence to the original story. If the order is different, ask the students to explain why.

Editorial Cartoons

Editorial cartoons can be funny or serious. They can include an activity, commentary, title, dialogue, or just the artist's thoughts on a subject. Cartoons can add details that help tell a story or explain a situation, event, or experience. To give them some insight into editorial cartoons, have students gather some from newspapers and magazines that concern the issue, situation, event, or experience being covered. What point is each cartoon trying to make? Then, based on your unit of study, do some brainstorming to create a list of situations and events that could make for some interesting cartoons. For example, if you were studying the Book of Genesis, a list of cartoons based on the story of Jacob and Esau could look something like this:

Jacob before his father Isaac
Esau standing in the kitchen
Jacob and Rachel conspiring
Isaac giving a blessing
The family getting together
Jacob and the ladder

The kids can work either individually or in groups to create a book of editorial cartoons for the whole class to enjoy.

Student-Created Encyclopedia

Tell the students they are to pretend they have been asked to create an encyclopedia of their studies. Give each student or pair of students, depending on the size of your class, a letter of the alphabet. Ask them to find a topic that is part of your unit of study and that begins with the letter. Remind students that being a writer for an encyclopedia means they must write everything they know about the subject. This will get them to think and to conduct some research to find out all they can about their subject. Students can rummage through newspapers, magazines, reference and resource books, and even encyclopedias to gather their information. As they gather their materials, students write articles, creating illustrations as necessary to include in their portion of the encyclopedia. Be sure the articles have bylines and are arranged in alphabetical order. Have students design a cover, as well as a title page that informs people who created this product.

This is *not* a one-day lesson. Rather, this activity can go on for a number of sessions—even the entire year, and the completed product will be a closure for what students have learned throughout the year.

Not the Same Old Book Reports!

Here are a series of activities you can do with children after you have read a story related to your unit of study:

Through the Eyes of a Story Character

Each child makes a mask to represent the character whose role he or she wants to take. Then, wearing the mask, the child takes on the role of this character. He or she can tell how it felt while the action was taking place or retell the story from his or her character's point of view.

Story Becomes Art

This will require the students to really work together but will reinforce a story's message. Assign each student a section of the story. You will need drawing paper for each student, along with markers or crayons. The drawing paper will need to be the same size and be laid out in the same direction.

Tell the students they are going to illustrate the different sections of the story. They will have to coordinate their drawing with those who are drawing on the right and left sides so they match the flow of the story. Be sure the edges of the paper match. Upon completion of the drawings, hang the pictures in story order. As each picture is hung, the artist retells that part of the story.

Talk to a Character

The students choose a character with whom they would like to have a conversation. Before they begin any conversation, however, the students should make notes of what they want to talk about. The students can also imagine how a character might respond, what expressions he or she might use, and so on. The students begin the conversation by writing down what the two people might say.

Add a Paragraph

Students can put themselves into the story by adding a short paragraph or two to the action. For example, in the middle of the action, the main character's mother might walk in and say, "Shabbat is about to begin." Students imagine being with the character at this moment. They respond in their own voice to the events and take part in the Shabbat in the story. The students then write what will take place when this happens.

Jar of Riddles

Kids love riddles. Get a jar and strips of brightly colored paper. Prepare riddles. There are some Jewish books of riddles available to make it easier for you, but here are a few to give you an idea of how easy it is to create your own:

- What has a lid, holes and smells good? *[spice box]*
- I was born in Poland but came to Palestine, where I declared the establishment of Israel in 1948. Who am I? *[Ben-Gurion]*
- I'm full of water but you wouldn't want to drink me. *[Dead Sea]*

You could also have the students create their own riddles to help fill the jar.

Jewish Catalogs

This can be a year-long project with a product at the end of the year. Show the students some mail-order catalogs. Include if possible copies of different Jewish catalogs. Let students' creative imagination go to work as they design the format for their own Jewish catalog. As you teach different topics, set aside time during each lesson for students to create a related catalog page. For example, you could have bolts of fabric or dream catchers for the Joseph story. Have plenty of scrap paper available so students can lay out each page. Finished pages can be kept in a folder; at the end of the year, students put the pages together and design a cover. It is also a good way to keep a record of the school year's activities.

Crazy Fun Puzzles

Prepare a small word search grid. Scatter the letters of an object, concept, or event (for example, m-e-z-u-z-a-h). Fill in the grid with more letters, two each. Do not use the letters of the word you want children to identify. Copy and pass out to the students. Tell the students to cross out all the letters that appear twice and unscramble the remaining letters. When they have done that, let them tell you the word they find. What is it? What does it mean? What does it represent? How do you use it? Of course, the questions you ask will depend on the word you choose.

Another Crazy Puzzle

Prepare a picture of something that reflects your unit of study, but leave something out of the picture so there is a big blank space. Copy and give out to the students. Tell them to fill in the part of the picture that is missing. Give them time to complete, then see what they have placed in the blank space. Invite students to explain their choices to the class.

Sacks of Introduction

When you are going to introduce a new concept, idea, moment in history, city in Israel, person, and so forth, take a paper sack and decorate it in an attractive manner to catch the eyes of the students. Place inside the sack those items that are most important to your unit of study. Use pictures if necessary. Give the students clues about what is in the sack. As they guess an item correctly, take it out and explain (or have students try to explain) how it relates to the unit of study. Continue until all the items have been identified.

Junior and Senior High School

The Bible and Other Jewish Texts

Identify Something Specific

Give the students something specific to identify as they read the text. For example, divide the class into small groups and give each group a short text portion to read. Also give the group a question. For example, a group assigned Genesis 1:1–5 might be asked to identify one sentence that would explain what is unique about the beginning and ending of Jewish days.

> "And there was evening and there was morning, a first day," teaches us that the day begins with evening and follows with the morning.

Other examples:

Genesis 2:4–7 (God creates man): Of what was Adam created, and what choices do humans have as a result?

Genesis 2:18–24 (God creates woman): What did God take from Adam to create a woman, and how does this affect the relationship between man and woman?

After each group has read and discussed its assigned text, ask each group to share its findings.

Another Approach

That is one approach, but here is something else to consider. You can also use questions that relate the text to the student's own personal life experience. For example, recently I worked with my granddaughter to help her understand the Torah portion for her bat mitzvah so she could write her speech. Her Torah portion was *Shoftim,* which contains the well-known statement, "Justice, Justice shall you pursue" (Deuteronomy 16:20). We read the text, and I used some general questions to get her thinking. Then I said: "Tell me all the things you can think of that are unfair to you or in your life." Once she got started, she ended up with quite a list of items. We talked about them all, relating them to the text, and brought her list down to two items that she felt very strongly about. One dealt with cheating, and the other was about judging others. I provided her with some midrashim that related to the text and her choices. By the time we finished, she was able to write her speech because she really understood her Torah portion.

One more comment about teaching Torah: *The Torah is more than the story and history focus we are accustomed to; it is also a legal and cultural document.* As Rabbi David Wolpe notes in *Teaching Your Children About God,* "When we read the Bible we want to show how real people overcome difficulties, not that they never have them."

BIBLE STUDY

Biblical Scavenger Hunt

Here is a fun way to help students learn to navigate the Bible. Your scavenger hunt can relate to your unit of study, or it can be a tool for studying the weekly Torah or haftarah portion. Make up a list of questions you want students to answer or verses you want looked up. For example, a scavenger hunt for Balak (Numbers 22:2–25:9) might include the following:

1. What chapters make up *Parashat Balak? [Numbers 22–24]*
2. What verses tell us who Balak is and of what nationality? *[22:2–4]*
3. What does Balak say in Numbers 24:5? Where else have you seen this verse? *[How fair are your tents, O Jacob, your dwelling places, O Israel; in the siddur.]*

This activity can be done by students individually, in pairs, or in small groups. You can also have students make up their own biblical scavenger hunts.

Putting Text to Work

An important aspect of text study is to be able to take some sort of action that reflects a major concept from the text. For example, in Genesis 24:1–20, part of *Parashat Chayei Sarah,* Abraham sends his servant on a mission to find a wife for Isaac. The servant develops a scheme to identify the right woman: she must not only offer him water at the well, but must also go beyond that and perform another act of *g'milut chasadim* by watering his camels, as well.

Read the text. Discuss with the students the plan that the servant developed. What was it? How did it help the servant find the right woman? Emphasize the importance of the acts of loving-kindness in identifying the right woman. Now, divide the class into small groups. Ask them to first define their idea of *g'milut chasadim.* Students then are to make a list of what they consider to be the top ten acts of *g'milut chasadim.* They are also to discuss the differences between random acts of kindness and *g'milut chasadim.* After the groups have shared their definitions of *g'milut chasadim* and compared it with random acts of kindness, make a composite list of the students' top ten on the board. As a closure, ask the class to choose one act of *g'milut chasadim* that the class could perform together. Then make plans to complete the task.

Let's Look at the Covenant

Divide the class into small groups. Prepare sheets with the texts of Genesis 1:26–31 and Genesis 9:1–11, or use the actual Bible and assign these portions. Have students read the two texts. Start off with some general questions. Additional questions that also can be used for discussion include the following:

What are the differences and similarities between these two Torah texts?
What does God give Adam and Eve to eat?
What additional food was given to Noah and his sons?
What restrictions are placed on the "flesh" of what they can eat?
What are the reasons for these restrictions?
How are these restrictions fulfilled today?
What does it mean to have "dominion" over every living thing?
What responsibility does this place on the individual person?
What have you done to accept this responsibility?

Is Genesis 1:26–31 a covenant? What is missing?

Why do you think it is missing?

If God is establishing a covenant through Noah and his descendants, why is Noah not considered one of the patriarchs?

From the conditions of the covenant, so far, which ones do you find easy to follow?

How do you follow them today?

What are your reasons for finding them difficult?

Abraham's Covenant

Either as a continuation of the previous activity or as a separate one, have students read Genesis 17:1–11, either in the Bible or from a handout. Use the following questions to guide the discussion.

What will Abram become when God tells him his name is changed to Abraham?

Who is to maintain the Covenant with God?

Until now there have been individual tribes. What change is taking place with the announcement by God of the Covenant?

What benefits are derived from being part of a community that lives, works, and prays together?

What influence has the Covenant with God had on the Jewish people?

In what ways has it helped the Jewish people to survive?

What do you think you can do to keep the Covenant alive today?

The Ten Commandments

One version of the Ten Commandments can be found in Deuteronomy 5:6–18. Copy the text for the students or use Bibles. Have the students read this version, then talk about how the Ten Commandments can be divided. Point out that they are usually broken into several sections, beginning with a preamble: "I the Lord am your God." Then comes a review of past favors: "Who brought you out of the land of Egypt, the house of bondage." The first part refers to a human's relationship with God, while the last part has to do with one person's relationship to another. The Ten Commandments are often considered the terms of the Covenant. Discuss the reasons for this with students.

After reading the Ten Commandments, ask the students to individually finish a few incomplete sentences with the first words that come to mind, for example:

The Covenant is important to the Jewish people because . . .
I can remain faithful to the Covenant by . . .
I can be a partner with God by . . .
Today, the Covenant means . . .

Have the students write their responses to the incomplete sentences. The reason is not to keep the response private, but to allow students to think about their answers. Upon completion, ask them to share their responses.

Another Approach to the Ten Commandments

After they receive the Ten Commandments, the Israelites say, "All that the Lord has said, we shall do and obey" (Exodus 24:7). What does this mean for students today? Prepare and distribute to students the following questionnaire:

First Commandment: We only have the use of human language to describe our belief in God.
Sometimes it is totally inadequate, but if we are to be partners with God, there has to be a belief in the Jewish God-idea—whatever it might be. Describe your Jewish God-idea.

Second Commandment: Make a list of the various ways people bow down to other gods today. It could apply to things that are more important to people than spiritual rewards. How many, from your list, apply to you personally?

Third Commandment: Identify some of the different ways we "swear falsely by the name of God" today. How many of those identified apply to you?

Fourth Commandment: What are some of the major concepts of humanity this commandment recognizes? How do you make Shabbat a very special day in your life?

Fifth Commandment: What are some ways you can honor your parents? Describe some of the "sins against one's household" taking place today. How do these sins affect one's neighbors?

Sixth Commandment: "Murder" can mean more than just killing someone. What are some other ways we "murder" a person?

Seventh Commandment: If adultery and idolatry are forms of infidelity, what other forms of infidelity are there?

Eighth Commandment: Identify everything you can think of that we steal from one another. What efforts can you make to not steal?

Ninth Commandment: What does "bearing false witness" mean? Describe how it is done in today's world. How can we avoid bearing false witness?

Tenth Commandment: What belongings of your neighbors or friends have you coveted? Are you really satisfied with what you have? How can you satisfy your desire?

After students have had a chance to complete the questionnaires, invite students to share their responses.

Parashat Mishpatim

Some texts lend themselves well to a teaching activity. One such text is *Parashat Mishpatim.*

Mishpatim follows immediately after the giving of the Ten Commandments in *Parashat Yitro.* The first question for the students to consider when beginning this lesson should be: Why do all these laws immediately follow the giving of the Ten Commandments? Give the students a chance to respond to this question. (The Sages say that it is to show that the Ten Commandments are not the only laws found in the Torah. These laws in *Mishpatim* are just as important as the Ten Commandments, and to show their importance they follow the giving of the Ten Commandments.) Have a copy of the Torah for each student, or distribute copies of the texts for Exodus 21:1–37, 22:1–30, and 23:1–19.

With the students talk about:

Receiving the Ten Commandments
More laws to consider in this *parshah*
Most of these laws fall into the realm of human logic and reason; talk about the meaning of these two words so students understand.

Divide the class into small groups of three or four, then tell them: Your task will be to read through the laws. As you read through the various laws, consider: What is the law teaching us? What is the spirit of the law? What is the law's ethical and moral boundaries?

As students read, they are to complete these three tasks:

1. Determine which category—moral, religious, or civil—each law belongs to and place it in its proper category. (*Note:* A law may fit more than one category.)
2. For as many laws as possible, identify how that law applies to us today. How does it fit into our current society?
3. For each law, or as many as possible, write a modern or contemporary version.

Allow time for the students to complete their tasks, then ask for sharing from each group. Be sure to compare the differences and similarities among each group's category assignments. Compare also how each story defined the laws for today. This could also be a good time for discussion among the groups because of their different interpretations. Allow for the differences and be sure the students are accepting of one another's ideas.

Students Become Bible Commentators

Give the students a Torah portion like *R'eih* (Deuteronomy 11:26–16:17). This *parashah* deals with all the different kinds of *tzedakah* and mitzvot.

Divide the class into small groups. Assign each group a portion of the text to read, then see how many different mitzvot members can find mention of in their passage. Students should also determine how many different guidelines for giving *tzedakah* are included in the passage. Finally, Deuteronomy 15:4 says: "There shall be no needy among you." Have them explain the significance of this statement. Upon completion of their tasks the groups are to share their results. Compare the differences and similarities.

The Bible and Midrash

Midrashim can help the students understand portions of the Bible. As an example, here is one based on the very first sentence of the Torah, "When God began to create heaven and earth" (Genesis 1:1).

> Rabbi Menachem Mendel was a Hasidic rebbe who lived in Kotsk, Poland. One of his students, Rabbi Leibele Eiger, remembers this lesson that the Kotzker Rebbe taught about Creation. The Kotzker translated the first verse in the Torah as: "God created (only) the beginning of the heavens and the earth." Then he explained, "It is up to us to determine how they turn out. It is our job to finish Creation." The Jewish tradition refers to the job of finishing Creation as *tikkun olam*—meaning "fixing" or "finishing" the world.

Have the students list individually the top five things that we need to do to "finish Creation" and make the world right today. Have students share their lists; make one composite list as they do so. Ask the students to reach a consensus and develop a class "top five" list. From this list, have each student determine which one he or she feels able to do. If several students choose the same one, they can become a group.

Each group is to develop a program to carry out its efforts to repair the world. Give groups any necessary assistance. Encourage each group to involve as many people as possible in the project. Students will have learned a little Torah and, also, will have begun to put their learning into action!

The Book of Ruth

We often do not get to the Book of Ruth when teaching our students because it is read during Shavuot, and often religious school has ended for the year by then. But Ruth is a beautiful book that describes many deeds of loving-kindness, a number of which pertain to Ruth's being a stranger in a strange land and how she is accepted. The Book of Ruth contains many good lessons for the students, no matter the time of the year. What follows is an introductory activity to the Book of Ruth.

Stranger in Our Midst

Divide the class into small groups. Each group is to design a three-minute skit based on one of the following:

A new person tries to enter a group.
A stranger is chosen last for a group.
A stranger is kept out of the group.
A stranger is made to feel welcome.
A stranger is made to feel unwelcome.

Give the students ten minutes to prepare, then have each group present its skit. After each performance, ask students:

What kind of behavior did you see?
What feelings were expressed?
When did you yourself ever feel that way?

After all the skits have been presented, ask the class: Have you ever gone up to a complete stranger in your synagogue and introduced yourself?

Now, read the story of Ruth, then discuss the following:

What did Ruth do to be accepted in her new community?
What do you do to be accepted by others?
What was done to make Ruth feel welcome and more at ease in her new community?
What do you do to make a stranger feel welcome?
Identify the deeds of loving-kindness of Ruth, Naomi, and Boaz.
What can we learn from the story of Ruth about how to treat strangers?
What one thing are you willing to do to be more accepting and understanding of the stranger in our midst?

The Prophet Ezekiel

Ezekiel is one prophet that most teachers avoid only because he seems to be difficult to understand. In fact, the ancient rabbis used to say a person should not study the beginning and end of Ezekiel until he had reached the age of thirty. With all the interest today in Kabbalah and Jewish mysticism, the prophet Ezekiel could be of interest to the students. He is thought of as a strange figure of fantasy, but he made major contributions to Jewish life at the time. Ezekiel's visions provide evidence of a very early form of Jewish mysticism, known as *Merkabah* mysticism. *Merkabah* mystics perceived God's appearance on a chariot. One of the contributions that Ezekiel made can be understood by reading the following portions of the Bible: Exodus 34:6–7 and Ezekiel 18:2–3, 20. These verses have to do with the "sins of the fathers" being visited upon the children. Distribute copies of these verses to students. After reading the Exodus quote, divide the class into small groups. Have them make a list of all the "sins" of our ancestors that are visited upon the children. Upon completion of this task, have groups share the lists, and make one composite list on the board.

Then, read Ezekiel 18:2–3 and do some brainstorming with the students, asking such questions as:

How many different ways can you think of where parents sow and children reap sour grapes?

How many different ways are children judged on the basis of their parents' attitudes, attributes, or activities?

What do parents, knowingly or unknowingly, transfer to their children?

Now, read the final selection, Ezekiel 18:20, which negates the Exodus concept of visiting the sins of the fathers on the children. Discuss with students:

What are the similarities and differences between the three biblical quotes?

How does society impart responsibility?

What responsibilities today do parents have for their children? Give examples.

What responsibilities do children have for their own actions? Give examples.

At what age should a child be responsible for his or her own actions? Give examples.

How do we learn to be responsible individuals?

What can we do to ensure our sins are not visited on our children?

Descriptions of Leaders in the Torah and Midrash

The Bible and various midrashim do give some good ideas of the role of a leader. These can be used whenever you have an election going on: the students can compare a leader's role in Jewish life with that of a leader in secular life, for example:

Let the Eternal, the God of the soul of all flesh, pick a person to lead the community, one who will go out before them and will return ahead of them—who leads them out and brings them back—for the community of the Eternal will not be like a flock without a shepherd. (Numbers 27:16–17)

Moses says "God of the soul of all flesh" to show us that like God, a good leader must be able to reach each and every person individually and on their terms. (Rashi, midrash on Numbers 27:16–17)

Make a list of the strong points of a leader as mentioned in these quotes, then compare these strong points with the current candidates who are now running for election, to whatever office. Students discuss how the different candidates are showing their ability to lead. How are they meeting the needs of the individual? What other needs of the individual could be met but are not at the present? Let the students determine who would be the better candidate, based on the Jewish description of a leader and their own discussion.

OTHER TEXTS

A Bit of Talmud

Don't panic—you use the Talmud more than you think! You *can* teach Talmud, or at least an introduction to it. In fact, you actually use it quite often, even if you're unaware of that. A good portion of the Passover Haggadah is derived from the Talmud. *Pirkei Avot* is also from the Talmud. What follows is an example of a lesson based on *Pirkei Avot* 2:9, which reads:

> [Rabbi Yochanan] said to [his students]: "Go out and see which is a good path for a person to attach oneself to. Rabbi Eliezer said, "*Ayin tovah*—a good eye." Rabbi Yehoshua said, "*Chaver tov*—a good friend." Rabbi Yossi said, "*Shachen tov*—a good neighbor." Rabbi Shimon said, "One who foresees the outcome of one's actions." Rabbi Elazar said, "*Lev tov*—a good heart." He [Rabbi Yochanan] said: "I prefer the words of Rabbi Elazar, for included in his words are your words."

Distribute copies for students to read, then discuss. You can use such questions as:

What made Rabbi Yochanan send his students to find out which path to follow?
What is the difference between the right path to follow and characteristics of an individual?
Which would you consider the best path to follow?
Which is the best characteristic?

Be accepting of all their answers. You may wish to share your opinions, but be sure they are labeled as such.

Next, on the chalkboard, or using five separate large sheets of newsprint, place the following headings:

A good eye
A good friend
A good neighbor
One who foresees the outcomes of one's actions
A good heart

For each item, do some brainstorming, making a list of its value and how it could lead one on the correct path in life. Keep in mind that "path" can also refer to characteristics. What character traits are best used to obtain the "correct" path? Consider using such questions as:

What can a "good eye" (or "good friend," and so on) see?
What would the relationship of a "good eye" have to a character trait?
What is the value of a "good eye"?
How would a "good eye" help one to follow the correct path?
What character traits are involved in following the "correct path"?
Given what you have studied, what is the "correct path"?

Once the students have made lists for each item, do some comparing. What are the similarities and differences? What reason would there be for the choice of the correct path's being the good eye? a good friend? a good neighbor (and so on)? To finish, sum up what students have said. Did they reach a consensus?

Ours or Theirs?

When it comes to Passover, most of the kids know all about the plagues and the different prohibitions of food, but few know about what God tells the Israelites to do to get ready to leave Egypt after the tenth plague. Either have a copy of the Torah for each student, or copy Exodus 11:1–3 and 12:35–36 and hand out to the students. Briefly, this is the portion of the Torah where God says to Moses: "Tell the people to borrow, each man from his neighbor and each woman from hers, objects of silver and gold." The children of Israel do as Moses tells them. The upshot is that when the Israelites leave Egypt, they take all the gold and silver with them. The Sages say that God's commandment to "borrow" from the

Egyptians was to fulfill the promise made by God to Abraham more than four hundred years earlier: "Your children will be enslaved and afflicted for four hundred years in a land that is not theirs. And the nation whom they will serve I will judge and afterward they will come out with great wealth" (Genesis 15:13–14).

Have the students read the Torah portion. Then, relate to them the story from the Talmud (*Sanhedrin* 91a) concerning the silver and gold that the Israelites borrowed from the Egyptians found on the handout on p. 96. (You may wish to copy and distribute.)

Stop after the first paragraph and ask the following:

What do you think?
Should the "borrowed" gold and silver be returned? What are your reasons for your answer?
What right did the Israelites have to "borrow" the gold and silver?
Have you ever borrowed something? How long did you keep it before you returned it?
Did the person you borrowed it from have to come after you for the item?
What right did you have to keep it so long?

Let the discussion continue so everyone has an opportunity to participate. You could even have a debate on whether the Jews should return the gold and silver; reasons why they should or shouldn't return it, and so forth. See what the students' decision will be, and be sure they state the reasons for the decision.

After you have finished the midrash discuss with students how their results compared with the end results from the midrash. Then ask students: Do you think the Israelites ever considered returning the gold and silver? Was it just payment for all their labors? Or was their borrowing similar or different from one asking to "borrow a match" which is used and never returned?

Jewish History

What Is History?

Students will find out that not all history is written down in the books. It can begin at home, with their becoming the actual historians.

Talk with the students about how history is recorded. Elicit from students that every day is a bit of history, and we find it on television and in newspapers and magazines. Have students ask their parents to share a story about some event that happened (bar/bat mitzvah, broken arm, sports award) or that affected them

HANDOUT

"Ours or Theirs?" Activity

When Alexander the Great conquered the Middle East, the Egyptians brought their case before him and demanded that the gold and silver, which the Jews had borrowed from their ancestors upon leaving Egypt many years earlier, be returned. A Jew by the name of Geviha ben Pesisa, who was not a great scholar, asked the Sages for permission to plead the Jewish case before Alexander. "If I lose, you can argue that they triumphed over a mere amateur. If I win, you can justifiably say that it was the Torah that won!" he said. The Sages agreed.

At the trial, the Egyptians presented their claim before Alexander. Geviha then asked the Egyptians, "Do you have proof to substantiate your claim?"

"Yes, we do, from your Torah," they replied. They quote the passage of the Torah: "The children of Israel did as Moses told them and they borrowed of the Egyptians jewels of silver and jewels of gold. And God gave the people favor in the eyes of the Egyptians and lent them."

"In that case," Geviha replied, "I, too, will answer you with proof from the Torah. The Torah states that more than 600,000 Jews were enslaved by your ancestors. Pay us the wages owed to 600,000 Jews for hundreds of years of hard labor and we will return the gold and silver we borrowed."

Alexander told the Egyptians to reply. They requested three days to answer. In the end, when they realized that having to pay for the labor of 600,000 people for all those years would be a much greater amount, they dropped the case and fled.

(Yom Kippur War) when they (the parents) were kids. Students can find out where their parents came from, where their grandparents were born, how holidays and life-cycle events were celebrated, and so on. Have students share their stories during the next class. Keep in mind that once the kids get started, one person's story just might remind another student of a story his or her parent related. Allow time for students to share all these stories. Ask students to compare the "old days" to today. Explain that such dialogue is oral history in the making.

Now, how about recording this oral history and making it something that can be kept and shared with others? Have students write down the stories they heard and compile the tales in a booklet. Oral history now becomes written history!

As you delve deeper into the study of Jewish history, remind the students of the process they went through. See if they can identify the way the history they are studying was recorded for preservation.

Zachor: Remember

This activity offers another way to introduce your students to the study of Jewish history. Begin by briefly sharing one or two of your own memories—something from your childhood, something one of your own parents did when young, or a special holiday celebration. Comment on the ways you keep memories about your ancestors alive and how important these memories are to you.

Give the students a few minutes to think about their own personal memories of holiday celebrations, special birthdays or events in their lives, and so on. Ask them to share these memories orally or to write down a list of memories on a sheet of paper. Ask students to leave their names off the sheets. Collect the papers, shuffle well, and read some of the memories. Talk about what makes such memories important to an individual.

Do some brainstorming, making a list of all the things that Jews remember, such as events that took place thousands of years ago (the Exodus), painful events (the Holocaust), glorious events (creation of the State of Israel), and so on. Discuss with the students: What makes the Jews continue to remember all these happenings? Why is it important to remember? Which is easier to remember: painful or glorious events? When you remember, does it sometimes make you feel more connected to the Jewish people? What are your reasons?

As a closure, ask the kids to make a list of events from recent history that they hope the Jews of the future will remember and commemorate. Write the list on the board for all the students to see.

A Personal Time Line

This activity will show the students that everyone has a personal history that is affected, to a certain extent, by the events and times in which he or she lives.

Discuss with the students a time line, its purpose, and how it can be used—not so much to memorize dates, but to see when events have taken place in their lives. Prepare a time line of your own life so students can see how one is developed. Then do the following:

1. Ask the students to take a sheet of paper and draw a horizontal line in the center. They are to place their birth date, including year, at one end and the current year at the other end of the line.

2. Tell them to think for a few minutes about different events that have taken place during their lives and then fill in the time line. Let them share their time lines when they have completed it.

3. Draw a time line on the board. Taking the birth year of the oldest students in the class, place it at the beginning, with the current year at the end. Ask the students to contribute major events that have taken place, using their own time lines for reference. Include Jewish social, historical, and cultural events, as well as secular events, along with any economical, political, and military milestones that they can think of.

4. Upon completion of the class time line, discuss with the students how these events have had an impact on their lives. In what way were the students affected by the events that have taken place?

5. For homework, ask the students to interview their parents to find out what historical events took place during their lifetime. During the next class, the students can list the responses on a "Parents' Time Line" on the board.

6. Discuss what impact the events had on the lives of their parents. What did their parents have to say about the changes that have taken place?

7. Now, make a time line of Jewish history. Since that could be quite long, I suggest you focus on, say, two or three decades. Take a look at the major events that have taken place. Let the students add any missing events that they think might have had an impact on the Jewish people. Talk about the impact the events on the time line had with the Jews. How did the events impact students' own lives? The message: everyone has a personal history that is affected in some way by the times in which we live!

HISTORY OF ISRAEL

Jerusalem through the Ages

Divide the class in small groups. One group at a time, let the students loose in the library to do some research. (*Note:* You may want to have an aide or parent help out in the library.) Students are to find as many different names for Jerusalem as they can. (For your information, there are seventy!) Students are to list the name, what period of time this name was used, the name of the ruling country during this period of time, and what the Israelites were called. Give each group the same amount of time. To present the information, ask the group to create a collage poster listing the various names and all the information. Upon completion, each group makes a presentation. See how many names the groups have discovered. You can find this information, by the way, in a book called *Whose Jerusalem?* by Eliyahu Tal—that is, of course, if you can't find it on the computer.

Alternative

If there is not time to make collages, have the groups come together to present their information. Make a composite list of names. Discuss where some of these names came from. Finally, have students vote on their favorite name for Jerusalem.

Creating News from the Past for Jerusalem

Divide the class into small groups. Depending on how many groups you have, give each group two or three of the following twelve historical periods of Jerusalem:

King David's conquest
Solomon's reign and the construction of the First Temple
First Temple period
Second Temple period
Bar Kochba revolt
Byzantine period
Islamic Jerusalem
Crusaders and the Ayyubid Dynasty
Mamluks
Ottoman Empire
British Mandate

State of Israel

Six-Day War

Ask the groups to search out some facts about each of the assigned periods of time. Have members consider the following:

Of what religion were the rulers at that time?

What religious traditions developed during the period?

What was taking place in the neighboring lands and how did this affect Jerusalem?

What influence did the rulers and events of this period have on the Jewish people?

Were there any adverse circumstances that affected the life of the Jews?

Once the research is complete, have each group create a separate newspaper for each time period that covers the information members have discovered. Include front-page headlines, articles, feature stories, the weather, human interest stories, and the like. Their newspaper can be placed on large butcher paper or newsprint for display purposes. Students should write as if they were actually part of the event. Post the completed newspapers around the room and have each group share its findings, using the newspapers as a guide.

After the presentations have been made, have the students compare the life of the Jews during the different periods to that of the Jews today. What are the similarities and differences? Examine the outside influences of the past and those of today. What are the similarities and differences?

THE HOLOCAUST

You have the choice of listing the facts about the Holocaust, or being a bit more creative in your presentation. To introduce the Holocaust and provide background information for the period, you could invite a Holocaust survivor. There are also many documentaries and films about the Holocaust. An extensive list can be found at **www.jewishfilm.com**.

Holocaust: Hatred, Ethnic Prejudice, and Discrimination

When studying the Holocaust, one area of importance to cover is prejudice, discrimination, and senseless hatred. Discuss with the students senseless hatred. What would they consider to be some examples of this? Make a list of their examples. Then make a list of what can be done to overcome this hatred, placing students' ideas next to the appropriate example. How do students deal with these feelings of hatred? How would they handle their hatred without hurting anyone? What is the difference between dislike and hatred? What do students like and dislike? What do they hate? (These questions are not in any particular order, they have just been presented for you to consider what to ask the students.)

Alternative

Hitler's "Aryan race" theory resulted in the deaths of millions as he made the effort to perpetuate the Aryan race because of his "hatred" of Jews and others. For another approach to introducing this subject divide the class into small groups. Tell each group to develop a three-minute skit that shows some type of hatred, prejudice, or discrimination. Keep in mind that what students create will probably reflect their own experiences, and this will give them a chance to deal with their feelings about these kinds of situations.

Let each group present its skit, and discuss the situations with the students after each presentation. After the skits and discussion, students are to research Hitler's "Aryan race" theory and discuss first its basic ideas within the group and then the flaws in Hitler's argument. Compare Hitler's theory to some of the current examples of prejudice and discrimination prevalent today. How are they alike? How are they different? As a final activity talk about what action students can take today in these kinds of situations.

Letter Writing During the Holocaust

Once you've begun your unit on the Holocaust, divide the class into small groups. Give each group a different event of the Holocaust, for example, Kristallnacht, the Wannsee Conference, the Warsaw Ghetto Uprising. Each group is to write two letters. One should be from a Jew living in Germany or an occupied country during the event. The other letter should be from the person who received the first letter responding to the person who is actually experiencing the conditions of the event. The letters are to contain the correct facts, yet students can add their own feelings and emotions about what they are encountering. Remind the students the letters are to be written as though they (the students) are living during this period.

HISTORY OF REFORM JUDAISM

The Platforms of Reform Judaism

Divide students into four groups. Assign each group one of the four different platforms of Reform Judaism: Pittsburgh, Columbus, the Centenary Perspective, and the Pittsburgh Principles of 1999. (These can be found at **www.ccarnet.org/platforms**.)

Ask each group to identify the outside influences at work during the period the assigned platform was created and to list all the major points. Have each group present its findings. Then, have them identify the following:

- The changes that have taken place from one platform to another.
- The similarities and differences among the various platforms.
- Events, discoveries, and so on that took place during the different time periods.
- The impact these had on the changes made in the different platforms.

Finally, have students make a list of any changes they think should be made in the next platform.

CURRENT EVENTS

History in the Making

Here are some brief activities that make use of events currently taking place. They help the students become actively involved in the making of Jewish history.

Identify a Newsmaker
Decorate a piece of poster board and place above it a sign saying: "Who Is This?" Mount a picture of a current Jewish newsmaker. See who in the class can identify the person and tell why that person is in the news.

Front and Center
Ask one student each week to take on the role of a famous Jewish newsmaker. After the student has studied the background of this person and the events concerning him or her, the student is to take center stage. The class can ask questions about the event and newsmaker's role in it. The student role-plays and defends that person's position and actions.

Making Lists

Ask the students to read the newspaper and identify issues of concern to the Jews: the environment, the Mideast and other conflicts, good deeds, and the like. Once a month, tell the students to take some time to make a list of all the news they remember reading about. Students then compare their lists and share the news items with one another.

Salute the Good Deeds

Have the students watch for those articles in the paper where someone has done something to help other people, save the environment, and so on. Ask them to collect the articles and bring them to school. You, or the students, prepare the bulletin board: place the articles, in an attractive manner, on the board. Before placing the articles on the board, ask the students to explain what was so special about what these people did and how it relates to Jewish values.

News Teams

Divide the class into small groups. Wherever possible, group together those who live in close proximity to one another. These groups become "news teams" that you assign a specific topic based on any current issues. These news teams gather their information during the week from newspapers and TV and radio newscasts, then prepare a "news team report" for the next class period. Assign one team to do the news per week. You might have to allow the students some time at the beginning of the class to get themselves organized, but they should have all their information gathered prior to the class.

Current Events Scavenger Hunt

Divide the class into small groups. Have complete sets of newspapers from different days of the week, one for each group. Prepare a list of what students are to find in their newspaper. Your list could look something like this:

Someone's success story
An event in Israel
The peace process in the Mideast

G'milut chasadim (deeds of loving-kindness)
An environmental issue
A story of concern to the group

Groups compile their stories and share them with the class.

News Flash!

As a homework assignment, the students are to prepare a news flash of an event that takes place during the week. Give them specific assignments or topics, for example:

The peace process in Israel
People helping people
Environmental issues
Animal stories
Life-saving stories
Health issues

For the news flash, each student writes a short summary of the information and draws an illustration of the event. Then, during class, pause from time to time for the students to deliver their reports. To make it even more realistic, prepare a large box by cutting out the front and decorating it to look like a television set. One more step: add Jewish content to the newsflash by asking: "What makes this a Jewish issue?" Discuss with the students the relationship of the story to our Jewish tradition.

The News as Part of Your Unit of Study

Decide what areas of the news you would like to emphasize. For example, if your unit of study includes Jewish values, divide your bulletin board into different sections: people helping people, environmental issues, animal care, medical ethics, and so on. Tell the students that during the week they are to watch the news on TV, writing a sentence or two about the news that applies to one of the different sections. Students also are to read the newspapers to find articles that relate to the different topics, bringing the articles to class and placing them on the bulletin board in the appropriate area. Then, as time allows, go over the articles. Where there is an area with just a few articles, or none, it is a good time to have a discussion about the lack of caring and what could be done about it. Your class could even develop a project that would make people more aware of the needs of the people, environment, or animal care, all based on Jewish values.

Examining World Leaders

Choose two Jewish people, or leaders of Israel and of the Palestinians; just be sure they are prominent in the news. Have the students look for similarities and differences in how the newspapers and media present these two people. Make a list of the positive and negative attributes the media and papers apply to each one. They can even collect photographs and cartoon caricatures from newspapers and magazines to identify the different ways these leaders are portrayed. Create a list of how these leaders are described. What kind of adjectives are used to describe them? When the students have gathered their material, share the results. The goal is to determine any bias that might persist in the media descriptions. Which leader is dealt with in a positive manner? Which one in a negative manner?

JEWISH HOLIDAYS

At this age, the students can take a more in-depth look at the holidays. They have had the rituals; now they can gain a better understanding of the meaning of the holidays. The following activities are for this purpose.

ROSH HASHANAH

What's Important to Me

There are twelve Jewish concepts within the Rosh HaShanah Shofar Service. They are:

Charity: "One who loves charity and justice causes the whole world to be filled with God's kindness." (Psalms 33:5)

Covenant: God said to Abraham, "You shall keep My covenant, you and your descendants after you, throughout their generations." (Genesis 17:9)

Faith: A man of faith will receive many blessings. (Proverbs 28:20)

Justice: Justice, justice, shall you pursue, that you may thrive and occupy the land that the Lord your God is giving to you. (Deuteronomy 16:20)

Mercy: The world is well conducted by two spinning wheels: one that spins justice and the other mercy. (*Zohar* 259b)

Prayer: When people pray, they should direct their hearts to heaven. (*B'rachot* 31a)

Redemption: Great is charity, for it brings redemption nearer, as it is said: Thus said the Lord: "Maintain justice, and practice charity, for My redemption is near and My lovingkindness is to be revealed." (Babylonian Talmud, *Bava Batra* 10a)

Remembrance: God heard [the enslaved people's] moaning, and God remembered the covenant with Abraham and Isaac and Jacob. (Exodus 2:24)

Repentance: Great is repentance for it brings healing to the world. (*Yoma* 86a)

Revelation: Rabbi Yochanan said: "Every sound of this complete revelation of the Truth that came from Sinai, was uttered in seventy languages." (*Shemot Rabbah* 28)

Shofar: God ascends midst acclamation; the Lord, to the blasts of the horn. (Psalm 47:6)

Sovereignty (of God): Thus said the Lord, the King of Israel, their Redeemer, the Lord of Hosts: "I am the first and I am the last, and there is no god but Me." (Isaiah 44:6)

Prepare a sheet with the above quotes. Then, gather together small pictures representing each of these concepts. There will be some concepts for which there is no actual "picture." So come as close to a representation as you can. For example, when I created this activity I used the following pictures:

Charity: a *tzedakah* box
Covenant: the Torah
Faith: Moses splitting the Sea of Reeds
Justice: a judge's gavel
Mercy: a dove with an olive branch
Prayer: a boy and girl with apples and honey
Redemption: Jonah inside the big fish
Remembrance: a *yarhzeit* candle
Repentance: a man blowing a shofar while a woman prays
Revelation: Moses with the two tablets
Shofar: a shofar
Sovereignty of God: the *Aron Kodesh*

Place the pictures randomly on a sheet of paper, with the "title" of each concept under the corresponding picture. Give students copies of this sheet, and also of the one listing the concepts and explanations so students can refer to it during this activity. Go over each concept with the students, discussing the different meanings of the words and pictures. Keep in mind that words and pictures have different meanings for different people. For example, charity is depicted by the *tzedakah* box, but charity doesn't always require giving money. *Tzedakah* means "righteous"; therefore, charity could also be a "righteous act."

After you have discussed all the concepts, give the students scissors, glue, and a sheet of 9 x 12 construction paper. Ask the students to cut the pictures out and decide which ones are the most important to them. Tell the students to place the concepts in order of importance to them on the construction paper, gluing the pictures in place when satisfied with the order. Upon completion, ask students to explain their choices.

Blowing the Shofar

Each Rosh HaShanah the shofar is blown, but do the students really know the reason for this event? The tenth-century scholar Saadyah Gaon gave us ten reasons for the sounding of the shofar during the Days of *T'shuvah* (repentance). Each reason reminds us of an important idea or event. These can be placed on the board, or you can print and copy them for the students. Read the reasons, one at a time. I have added questions after each reason for purpose of discussion. The questions can be used as is, or you can come up with your own:

1. Rosh HaShanah is celebrated as the beginning of Creation. We mark the celebration by proclaiming the sovereignty of God—God as Ruler of the whole universe.
   • Whatever your idea of God, how do you show respect for God?

2. The shofar serves a reminder to return to God; it stirs the people to repentance.
   • How do you repent for your sins?

3. The shofar reminds the people of the revelation at Mount Sinai.
   • What was revealed to the Israelites at Mount Sinai? What does it mean to you?

4. The shofar reminds us of the words of the prophets.
   • What can we learn from the words of the prophets?

5. The shofar reminds us of the destruction of the Temple in Jerusalem because the armies of this destruction sounded trumpet blasts as a battle cry.
    - What kinds of warning do we receive today when trouble is approaching?
    - How do we react to the warning?

6. When the shofar is sounded, the people tremble. (Amos 3:6)
    - What causes you to tremble?

7. The shofar reminds us of Isaac's sacrifice because a ram was substituted for Isaac as an offering to God.
    - As a Jew, how do you express your faith?

8. The shofar reminds us of the Day of Judgment.
    - For what do you want to say "I'm sorry"? Is saying "I'm sorry" enough?
    - What else could you do?

9. The shofar will herald the coming of the messianic age and the redemption of Israel.
    - What can you do to make a better world? better community? better home life?

10. The shofar reminds us of the traditional Jewish beliefs in resurrection of the dead and eternal life for the righteous.
    - What do you consider a righteous act?
    - What does "eternal life" mean to you?

The Three Parts of the Shofar Service

Now the students are ready to read the actual Shofar Service. Have High Holy Days prayer books for each student. Prepare the following handout for the students:

Three Parts of the Shofar Service

Read the following:

Maimonides says in the *Mishneh Torah* when the shofar is blown:

Awake, awake, O sleepers, from your sleep! O slumberers, arouse yourselves from your slumbers! Examine your deeds; return in repentance; and remember your Creator. Those of you who forget the truth in follies of the times, and go astray the whole year in vanity and emptiness, which neither profit or save, look to your souls. Improve your ways and works. Abandon, every one of you, the evil course and the thought that is not good. (Laws of Repentence 3:4)

- Talk about this statement. What is it saying to you?

In *The World of Prayer* by Rabbi Elie Munk the three parts of the Shofar Service are defined as follows:

- *Malchuyot* (Sovereignty): God as King of the present—the Master of all living things.

- *Zichronot* (Remembrances): God as Judge of the past—the Judge Who inquires into our Conduct.

- *Shofarot* (Revelation): God as Redeemer of the future—the Guide Who disciplines us and Teaches us God's laws.

According to tradition, each part of the Shofar Service is to contain ten verses from the Torah, Psalms, Prophets, and the final verse is from the Torah. Read the one verse below from each part. Using your High Holy Days Prayer Book, locate a similar verse within the corresponding part of the Shofar Service. Talk about the meaning of each part. What is it saying to you?

Malchuyot: The Eternal shall be Ruler over all the earth; on that day shall the Eternal be One and God's name be One. (Zechariah 14:9)

Zichronot: I will remember my covenant with Jacob; I will also remember my covenant with Isaac and my covenant with Abraham and I will remember the land. (Leviticus 26:42)

Shofarot: The shofar blast grew louder and louder; Moses spoke and God answered him. (Exodus 19:19)

Divide the class into small groups. Tell the students to follow the directions on the handout. Groups work together to identify the similar verses, then discuss their meaning within each group. A recorder should be appointed to take notes of the major points that come out of the discussion. Upon completion, ask the groups to share their results.

SHABBAT ACTIVITIES

The first time the Hebrew root k-d-sh, or "holy," appears in the Torah is in Genesis 2:3. God creates the world in six days, and then rests on Shabbat: "And God blessed the seventh day and made it holy." Everything God created during the six days of creation was "good," but when God comes to the seventh day (Shabbat), God says it is "holy." However, God didn't create a holy *place*—a mountain, a spring, a rock—where a sanctuary is established. According to Abraham J. Heschel in *The Sabbath,* the message of Shabbat is to celebrate time rather than space. Shabbat is a holy day set apart, a day that is unique in time. What follows are a series of different activities to help students appreciate Shabbat as a special, holy time.

The Essence of Shabbat

Prepare the following handout containing quotes about the Sabbath from Judaic sources. These are just a few of the many that are available. If you have some that you like better than these, use them!

The Essence of Shabbat
Artists cannot be continually wielding their brush. They must stop at times in their painting to freshen their vision of the object, the meaning of which they wish to express on their canvas. Living is also an art. We dare not become absorbed in its technical processes and lose our consciousness of its general plan. The Sabbath represents those moments when we pause in our brush work to renew our vision of this object. Having done so we take ourselves back to our painting with clarified vision and renewed energy.
(Mordecai M. Kaplan, *The Meaning of God*)

110

The seventh day is a palace in time which we build. It is made of soul, of joy and reticence. (Abraham J. Heschel, *The Sabbath,* pp. 14–15)

The Sabbath is a reminder of the two worlds—this world and the world to come, it is an example of both worlds. For the Sabbath is joy, holiness, and rest; joy is part of this world; holiness and rest are something of the world to come. (Abraham J. Heschel, *The Sabbath,* p. 19)

After reading, use the following questions as a guide for your class discussion:

What "picture" do you paint during the week?
How can the Sabbath let you renew or clarify your vision?
What colors fill your life during the week?
What colors are part of your life on Shabbat?
What premium do you place on time?
How do we lose time?
How can lost time be recaptured?
If we are building a "palace in time," what role or place does sadness have in Shabbat?
What brings you Shabbat joy?
What does Shabbat remind us from our Jewish heritage?
How essential is worship to Shabbat observance?
What makes community worship so important on Shabbat?
How can Shabbat strengthen family ties?
What would you be willing not to do on Shabbat to make it unique in your life?

The last question could be a closure for this activity. Or, hand out prayer books and ask each student to find one prayer within the book that expresses his or her "essence of Shabbat" and to share that prayer with the class.

Ten Commandments for Shabbat

This activity can be done with the class as a whole or in small groups, depending on how comfortable the students feel with one another. Prepare the following and distribute a copy for each student. Have the students read one commandment at a time, and then respond to the questions that follow it.

Note: Be sure students understand that these are ideals about Shabbat and are meant to be goals for us to strive toward. Do not condemn anyone's current Shabbat practices.

1. I am Shabbat that takes you out of bondage from lowly pursuits into the realm of life's highest values.
   - What "bondage" does Shabbat take you out of? What do you consider "lowly pursuits"? What are your "life's highest values"?

2. You shall have no other engagements on a Friday evening but home and synagogue.
   - What special plans do you make for Friday evening?

3. You shall not take the name of Shabbat in vain. You shall avoid all shopping, movie attendance, and other weekday pursuits.
   - What can you avoid doing on Shabbat that you do during the week?
   - What can you do on Shabbat that would be special for that day?

4. Remember Shabbat to keep it holy through worship, study, and cultural pursuits.
   - What can you do to make Shabbat holy?
   - What can you do to make Shabbat a special time in your home and with your family?

5. Honor the Jewish faith of your parent(s) by regularly attending Shabbat services.
   - What can you do to honor the Jewish faith of your parent(s)?
   - How often do you attend Shabbat services?
   - What can you do to attend more often?

6. You shall not kill the Sabbath spirit by engaging in work on Shabbat.
   - What is the Shabbat spirit?
   - How do you capture the spirit of Shabbat in your home?

7. You shall not be unfaithful to Jewish home life by banishing Shabbat candles and *Kiddush* from your home.
   - What is your Jewish home life?

- What do you do to make your home Jewish?
- What will you do to be faithful to Shabbat?

8. You shall not steal precious hours that belong to the synagogue and Judaism to engage in unworthy, unspiritual pursuits.
   - What do you do to make your Shabbat time precious to yourself and to your family?
   - What premium do you place on time? That is, how do you determine the value of your time?

9. You shall not bear false witness against the Jewish people by showing irreverence and unconcern for the Sabbath.
   - There are Jews in this world who cannot observe Shabbat. What responsibility do you have to observe Shabbat, if not for yourself, but for these people?

10. You shall not covet the pastimes of pleasure seekers who live as if Shabbat has no meaning and message for the modern world.
    - What message does Shabbat have for the modern world?
    - What message does Shabbat have for you?

As closure for this activity, ask each student to state at least one thing he or she would be willing to do on a regular basis to make Shabbat a special time.

Everything You Wanted to Know About the Sabbath!

Prepare the following questions about the Sabbath by placing each question on an index card and its answer on another index card. Or, you can place on letter-size paper and cut into strips after printing. Put the answers in one box and the questions in another. Be sure to mix them well so they are not in any order. A student draws a question from the question box, and another student draws from the answer box. Students need to decide if it is the correct answer (it probably won't be if everything is mixed well). The goal is to find the correct answer to each question. There are a lot of questions and answers, so I suggest you choose those you wish to use and use only the number needed for the size of your group. These questions can also be used as part of a scavenger hunt exercise where the students have to find the answers through research. Or these questions could be used for a review game like Jewish Jeopardy for playing after all these topics have been studied. *Note:* Each question is numbered and the answer is indented.

1. How is Shabbat considered the cornerstone of the Jewish religion?

    "And God blessed the seventh day and made it holy" (Genesis 2:3). As God sanctified the seventh day, so shall we.

2. Why is the seventh day called Shabbat?

    "And on the seventh day God ceased from work and rested" (Exodus 31:17 and Genesis 2:3). The Hebrew word *Shabbat* comes from the root meaning "stop" or "cease."

3. In which of the Ten Commandments is the observance of Shabbat ordained?

    In the fourth commandment. It is repeated twice in the Torah: "Remember the sabbath day and keep it holy" (Exodus 20:8) and "Observe the sabbath day and keep it holy" (Deuteronomy 5:12).

4. Why are there usually two candles lit on Shabbat?

    In honor of the two versions of the commandment regarding Shabbat in the Ten Commandments in the Torah. We shall "remember" and "observe."

5. Why are candles lit on Shabbat?

    In ancient times, the last work performed before Shabbat was preparation of the light. It became associated with the ushering in of Shabbat. Today it is a symbol of joy that fills the home on Shabbat.

6. When does Shabbat begin?

    It begins Friday evening, just before sunset.

7. How is one to honor the Sabbath?

    We honor Shabbat by making special preparations, removing signs of work and setting the home in order. We put aside mundane problems and dedicate ourselves to strengthening relationships with God, family, and fellow human beings.

8. What greetings are employed on Shabbat?

    "Good Shabbos" and "Shabbat Shalom!"

9. Is it true that only women can light the Shabbat candles?

    The Mishnah (*Shabbat* 11:5) counts this as one of the three commandments especially enjoined upon women. However, it is made clear that both men and women are commanded to make sure that the lights are kindled.

10. Why is the Shabbat bread called "challah"?

    The term "challah," which appears in Numbers 15:17–21, refers to the dough offering that every Israelite was required to present as a "gift to the Lord" whenever he or she baked bread during the time of the Jerusalem Temple. After the destruction of the Temple, Jews continued this practice for Shabbat and holidays and so the term challah was applied to these loaves themselves.

11. It is customary to place two loaves of challah on the Shabbat table. Why are there two loaves instead of just one?

    The two loaves commemorate the double portion of manna that the Israelites received in the wilderness on the eve of Shabbat (Exodus 16:22–30).

12. Why are the challot covered on the Shabbat table?

    The cover symbolizes the "fine layer of dew" that covered the manna (Babylonian Talmud *Yoma* 75b). In addition, meals usually are started with bread, but on Shabbat we start with wine. We cover the challah so it doesn't know that it's not first.

13. Why is it customary to sprinkle salt on the challah after the *Motzi?*

    This is done as a way of comparing the household table to the altar in the ancient Temple. As salt was sprinkled on the Temple offerings, salt can be used on the challah when the meal begins.

14. Why is *Kiddush* recited over wine at the beginning of the Shabbat meal?

    Kiddush, which means "sanctification," is a formal hallowing of the Sabbath. It is a benediction praising God for granting Shabbat to Israel as a perpetual heritage. Wine is used because it is a symbol of joy, and Shabbat is associated with joy.

15. What is the major purpose of all the Shabbat laws we find in the Torah and all the commentaries?

    The Shabbat laws lift the Jew out of the week's routine into a higher plane of existence where the Jew is free to think, feel, attain spiritual heights, and refresh the soul.

16. What is the difference between the two Shabbat commandments in
    Exodus 20:8 and Deuteronomy 5:12?
    The first says "remember" and the other says "observe."

17. Why do some Jews eat a fourth Sabbath meal on Saturday night?
    Many people preferred to have their main meal after *Havdalah* so
    they could have a freshly cooked meal. The meal was named *m'laveh
    malkah*, a farewell feast for the departing Queen Shabbat.

18. What is the name of the service that ends Shabbat and what does it
    mean?
    The ceremony is called *Havdalah.* It means "separation," from the
    holy and the profane: Shabbat and the weekday.

19. What is the *n'shamah y'tarah?*
    Legend has it that on Shabbat, every Jew is given an additional and
    more-exalted soul which remains with him or her throughout the
    day of rest.

20. What is the traditional hour for lighting the Shabbat candles?
    Because of the prohibition against kindling a fire once the Sabbath
    has begun, the candles are to be lit 18 minutes before sunset on
    Friday.

21. Why is Shabbat called "the bride"?
    According to the Talmud, God gave each day a mate; only Shabbat
    was alone. So God gave it to the people of Israel as Israel's mate, its
    bride.

22. What is meant by "Shabbat peace" or "Shabbat rest"?
    M'nuchah (rest) and *shalom* (peace) are more than merely rest and the
    absence of war, respectively. They express wholeness and harmony.
    On Shabbat, each person ceases completely to be an animal whose
    main occupation is to fight for survival and to sustain biological life.
    On Shabbat, our task is to be human.

23. According to traditional halachah, when is it permitted to disregard
    Shabbat observance?
    It may be disregarded when there is danger to human life.

24. What is the meaning of the different symbols used during a *Havdalah* service?

> The candle reminds us of the creation of fire for light. The spices keep the sweetness of Shabbat with us as we enter the week. Just as the drinking of the wine begins Shabbat, in the same way, the drinking of the wine marks the end of Shabbat.

25. Why is the *Havdalah* candle braided?

> Since the *Havdalah* candle reminds us of the creation of fire, the Rabbis taught that the *Havdalah* candle should have at least two wicks in order to stimulate fire. (Babylonian Talmud *P'sachim* 103b).

Students Learn About Shabbat on Their Own

There are aspects of the Sabbath to which some Jews give little thought; nonetheless they are important concepts in Jewish life. The concept of Sabbath peace is described in Jewish sources as a state of peace between human beings and nature. During the week, we create, but on the Sabbath we cease to interfere with the work of Creation—just as God created the world in six days and rested on the seventh day. The prohibition of work on the Sabbath has more to do with peace then it does with the mundane activity of work.

What the students could learn about Judaism from an in-depth study of the Sabbath:

Shabbat acknowledges human equality and dignity.
Shabbat affirms the humanity of the poor, the humble, the stranger, and the slave.
It arouses human consideration for all living creatures, animals included.
All social differences are annulled.
Shabbat banishes grief and sorrow (mourning is stopped on the Sabbath).
Shabbat is a reminder of our love of life, our joy of life.
If offers a taste of the world to come.

Divide the class into small groups. Give each group a different assignment to complete, such as the following:

1. Describe all aspects of forbidden Sabbath labor in traditional halachah and the reasons for its prohibition.

2. Describe the laws of social welfare we are to observe on the Sabbath and all who are involved in its observance.
3. Describe how the Sabbath affects every living creature.

The students are to gather their information. Give them time to work in the library.

Tell the students that once they have gathered all their information, they are to prepare a presentation that covers everything they have learned. Their presentation could be in any one of the following forms: a book with illustrations, a series of posters, a giant wall mural, a play, songs, a TV or radio newscast, or a video or slide presentation with script.

Give groups time to complete their work. Set aside time for each group to make its presentation to the class.

Jewish Values

God Concepts

The first thing the students have to consider is their concept of God. That, of course, means you must think about it as well. Remember to be accepting of students' views, even though those opinions might not be those you think kids should hold.

Here are two activities to consider.

"Sign" Language
Make the following signs:

Master of the Universe   God pulls strings. God controls the world, sets our future, and works miracles.

God as Watchmaker   A watchmaker puts a timepiece together, winds it up, and then leaves it running. Gods works in the same way: God created the world and then left it running.

God's Making a List   And God's checking it twice. God makes notes on what we do. Later, we'll get rewarded or punished for what we have done.

The Still, Small Voice   God is the voice that whispers in our ear—the feeling that we are doing something wrong or right. God is our conscience.

God Is Order   God is all the laws of nature and scientific truths. God is all the truths about man and woman, life, the world, the universe.

The Personal God—God Is Yours!   We have a personal relationship with God. God's presence comforts us and gives us strength.

God as the Ruling Spirit of the Universe   God is unseen; the unknown spirit that permeates the earth.

Place the signs around the room. Ask the students to read them carefully, then decide which one fits their idea of God the best—the one with which they can identify. Students are to go stand under that sign. Within the group—under the sign—they are to talk about the reasons for their choice. How did they arrive at their decision? What influenced them? What are the similarities and differences in how they arrived at their choice? Ask each group to choose a spokesperson for its group to share the responses with the class.

God-Ideas

This activity was created by Ellen Mack, an educator in Fort Worth, Texas. The list of God-ideas has been compiled from the book *Finding God: Selected Responses* by Rifat Sonsino and Daniel B. Syme. You can prepare this list as presented on a letter-size sheet of paper; or make up a set of index cards, with one God-idea on each card. You will need one copy of the list or one set of God-idea cards for each student in the class.

God-Ideas

Read through the following. Check off those with which you feel most comfortable:

___ 1. God is merciful, just, truthful, and compassionate.

___ 2. God is the image of man or woman's higher self, a symbol of what man or woman potentially is or ought to be.

___ 3. God is the symbol of our own powers, which we try to realize in our lives, and is not a symbol of force and domination.

___ 4. God is everywhere; there is nothing in which God cannot be found.

___ 5. God cannot be experienced; God can only be met through an encounter that defies description.

_____ 6. God cannot be defined by our human language.

_____ 7. We do not always open the doors leading to an encounter with God.

_____ 8. God is always present.

_____ 9. Human beings have a responsibility to join with God in the struggle of eradicating evil from the universe.

_____10. God is the combination of those forces in nature that help a human being reach self-realization.

_____11. God is the sum of everything in the world that renders life significant and worthwhile, or holy.

_____12. Prayer is taking inventory of ourselves, a reminder of who we are and what we can become.

_____13. Prayer is not a prayer to God, but becoming aware of God's presence as the Force sustaining the universe.

_____14. God is the pattern of perfection toward which we ought to strive throughout our lives.

_____15. God is the Energy, the Force, the Direction, the Thrust, out of which the universe has expanded and by which the universe is sustained.

_____16. God is the creative, spiritual seed of the universe.

_____17. God is power, a force operating within nature.

_____18. We work with God to reach the age of universal justice and peace.

_____19. God needs the help of human beings, and human beings need the help of God.

_____20. The powers of God are finite, bound by the limitations of existence.

_____21. God is not all-powerful.

_____22. God cares and deeply loves God's children.

_____23. God is all-good.

_____24. God hears and answers our prayers.

_____25. God is the Prime Mover in the universe.

_____26. God is all-knowing.

_____27. God is all-powerful.

_____28. God is One.

Give the students time to go over the list or to go through the deck of cards. Divide the class into small groups of three or four. Ask students to share their responses and talk about their similarities and differences. Remind students to listen to one another carefully and be respectful of one another's opinions. Bring everyone together and ask for volunteers willing to share their opinions. Which God-ideas were the most common to all the groups?

After the class completes one of these two activities, the next step is to bring prayer into the picture. This can be done in a number of ways. First, have prayer books for each student. Then ask children to do one of the following:

1. Find those prayers that reflect their God-idea.
2. Identify those prayers that praise God.
3. Determine which one prayer really fills their ideal of God.

Give students time to complete the activity, then invite them to share with the class what they have found. A simple closure for the day's lesson would be for each student to write a short prayer helping him or her reach for God, whatever the idea of God might be. This can be shared or placed in a journal.

Getting a grasp on their idea of God is a good beginning for the students as they study the prayers of our people.

Jewish Quotes for Jewish Values

Quotes can be used on a regular basis to inculcate Jewish ethics and values. Either you or your students can search out appropriate quotations.

Based on your unit of study, choose those quotations you think are most important for the students to learn. These quotes can become short, memorable lessons in Jewish moral and cultural literacy. Arrange them in an attractive manner on colorful poster board, large enough for the students to read easily. Hang the posters all around the classroom walls. Following are some quotes you can consider, but keep in mind that the quotes you choose should relate to your unit of study:

Let us walk in the light of the Lord. (Isaiah 2:5)
Love your neighbor as yourself. (Leviticus 19:18)
What is hateful to you, do not do to another. (Hillel, in Babylonian Talmud *Shabbat* 31a)
Do not wrong the stranger. (Leviticus 19:33)
Do not place a stumbling block before the blind. (Leviticus 19:14)
Who is wise? One who learns from everybody. (Ben Zoma, in *Pirkei Avot*, 4:1)

Leave the quotes up so the students become familiar with them. Repeated use of the quotes increases their impact; integrate them into you teaching.

Alternative

Have handy books of quotations, copies of *Pirkei Avot* and the like. As you proceed through your unit of study, ask the students to identify those Jewish quotes about Jewish ethics and morals that have meaning to them. They can make attractive posters using the quotes they like best and post them around the room.

An Example of What You Can Do with the Quotes

"Do not place a stumbling block before the blind" (Leviticus 19:14). As with most words from the Torah, there is more than meets the eye. Do some brainstorming with the students, making a list of all the ways this statement could be interpreted. Once the list is made, look at each statement and ask the following questions:

> How will this action help, hurt, or otherwise affect others than yourself?
> What would be the consequences to you or to others who would follow your example?
> What if others acted in the same manner?
> What would your parents, or the law, or Judaism say is right?
> What does your conscience tell you?
> What makes this fair?
> How different would you act if you knew the person?
> What questions of right or wrong are involved?

Such questions encourage the students to think about how their actions affect other people and to look beyond their own self interest and consider what is right and fair. By asking these clarifying moral questions, you will help young people to develop the habit of asking these kind of questions themselves.

A Jewish Values Auction

Jewish values are an important part of our heritage. Most of the time students are not aware of where these values come from. Like the random acts of Torah, the values are just there—there is no realization that those values are Jewish! With this activity, the students can have some fun while learning about "Jewish" values.

You will need to do a little preparation. First, identify the quotes from Jewish texts that speak of Jewish values. Make sure each quote corresponds to an important Jewish value. Here are a few examples to give you an idea of what to look for:

> Justice: Justice, justice shall you pursue. (Deuteronomy 16:20)
>
> Mitzvah: Greater is he who is commanded and carries out an act, than he who is not commanded and carries it out. (*Kiddushin* 31a)
>
> Respect for the oppressed: You shall not insult the deaf, or place a stumbling block before the blind. (Leviticus 19:14)
>
> Love of your fellow person: Do not say, "I will do to him what he did to me." (Proverbs 24:29)
>
> Honoring Parents: Honor your father and your mother, that you may long endure on the land. (Exodus 20:12)
>
> *T'shuvah*/Repentance: Repent one day before your death. Since no person knows the day of death, each person should repent every day. (*Shabbat* 153a)
>
> *Bikur Cholim*/Visiting the sick: Whoever visits a sick person removes one-sixtieth of his illness. (*Bava M'tzia* 30b)
>
> Respect for others: You shall not wrong a stranger or oppress him. (Exodus 22:20)
>
> *Tzedakah:* If there is a needy person among you, one of your kinsmen . . . do not harden your heart . . . [but] open your hand and lend him sufficient for whatever he needs. (Deuteronomy 15:7–8)
>
> *Pikuach Nefesh*/Preserving Life: Keeping the mitzvot means that you shall live by them and not die by them. (*Yoma* 85b)

Rather than searching through all the different books mentioned, use a book of Jewish quotations to quickly locate material.

The number of Jewish values on your list will depend on the number of students in your class. Have a few more than the number of students. Once your list is prepared, add space at the bottom of the page so that in the discussion that follows, students can make notes about the reasons for their value choices.

Make a List of Jewish Values

Divide the class into small groups. Tell each group it is to create a list of Jewish values. Students can use any resources they deem necessary to accomplish this task. Allow time for research or have books available. The Torah, of course, is a good source, as are midrashim, the Talmud, prayer books, and *Pirkei Avot*. When they have finished, have the groups share their lists. Make one composite list.

Give each student a copy of your list, as well as $2,000 in fun money.

Review each item on the list, discussing with the students what it means. Once you are sure students understand, ask them to check off those that are the most important to them. Of their most important, ask students to choose at least three that they would rank at the top. Have them write the reasons for their choices at the bottom of the paper. Now you are ready for the auction.

Go over the rules of the auction, then run it just like any auction you have ever seen. A student can buy more than one Jewish value, as long as the money holds out. Students are to keep track of their purchases. At the end of the auction, talk about what has taken place: How many were able to purchase any of their top choices? What made those choices so important to them? Give everyone a chance to talk—students will be excited about their purchases. The students will leave the class knowing a little more about themselves and their Jewish values.

Where Do You Stand?

In an article written for the winter 1997 issue of *Reform Judaism,* Arthur Gross Schaefer discusses "The Jewish Ethics Challenge: Where Do You Stand?" According to Schaefer, Who am I? and What do I value? are questions that deeply affect the decisions we make. He asks such questions as: What ethical values do we use when making decisions? Are they consistent with our obligations as Jews? How can Jewish values guide us in making tough decisions? Schaefer tells his readers to take the ethics challenge and see how their values compare with important Jewish considerations. Schaefer's article, including the challenge itself, can be found on the Internet at **www.urj.org/rjmag/1197ag.html**. Let the students take this challenge to see what their responses will be. When making their decisions, the students need to consider the following: the impact on others, other alternatives, and the core Jewish values involved. Point out to students that they will need to choose and prioritize: Of the core Jewish values, which are the most important? Of the options, which will do the greatest good? Only then should students make their decisions.

There are several sample situations presented in the article. In addition to the situations presented by Schaefer in his article, here are a couple of my own:

1. You like to buy and wear the current fashions with the names of the designers very prominently displayed. Recently, though, there have been a number of news stories about the poor compensation and factory work-

ing conditions. In addition, the stories say that young children are being hired to do some of the menial work. Do you:

   a. Decide not to buy the product.

   b. Decide not to buy the product and send a letter of protest to the company.

   c. Decide not to buy the product and enlist others in a boycott and letter writing campaign.

   d. Buy the product.

2. You go shopping with your friends at the mall. As you are all going home, one friend takes out a CD that she took from the music store. It is a very hot item, and she was very excited about having taken it—and gotten it for "free." Do you:

   a. Tell her to return it immediately.

   b. Tell your parents what your friend did.

   c. Tell your friend's parents what she did.

   d. Don't do anything and just enjoy listening to the music.

Now you can create some of your own situations!

Creating Mitzvah Booklets

There are, of course, lots of mitzvot one can do. However, for the purpose of this activity, I suggest you choose one specific area, such as relationships between one human being and another.

Do some brainstorming with the students, making a list of those Jewish values (mitzvot) that have to do with one's relationship to another such as:

Feeding the hungry
Visiting the sick
Caring for the orphaned, widowed, and homeless
Comforting the mourner
Showing kindness for strangers
Being honest in business dealings

After compiling the list, divide the class into small groups. Give each group one mitzvah. The group's task would be to:

1. Find one or two quotes from Jewish sources that tell us to perform this mitzvah. You may need to direct students to specific texts. Give them some library time to accomplish this part of the task.

2. Develop guidelines for performing the mitzvah. This could include what to do, when to do it, and how to do it. The group could also design a title page.

3. Compile each group's work into a booklet and copy so each student can have one. Make one copy to be placed in the synagogue library for use by members of the congregation.

Seek Peace and Pursue It

Gather together some quotes about peace from Jewish sources. Here are some to get you started.

> Rabbi Alexandri said: "Those who study Torah for its own sake make peace with all humankind." (Babylonian Talmud, *Sanhedrin* 99b)
> The disciples of the wise increase peace in the world. (Babylonian Talmud, *B'rachot* 64a)
> The work of righteousness shall be peace. (Isaiah 32:17)
> Seek peace and pursue it. (Psalms 34:15)
> When the mountains bear grain, the people enjoy peace. (*B'reishit Rabbah* 89:4)
> The need of charity is in its measure of kindness. (Babylonian Talmud, *Sukkah* 49b)
> Let not kindness and truth forsake you. (Proverbs 3:3)

Peace isn't the easiest thing to imagine in this day and age. There are a lot of small wars and other fighting taking place around the world, not just in the Middle East. Do some brainstorming with the students to make a list of all these conflicts. You could even include potential conflicts—minor events that may develop into major conflicts. Look at the list and see if the kids know anything about the causes of the conflicts. Make a note of the causes next to each one—help students with this if necessary; or, assign it as research, to be done before the next class session.

Post the Jewish quotes on the board, covering them until you are ready to use them. You can choose one quote to begin the process. Probably the most well known is "Seek peace and pursue it." Show this quote to the students and do some brainstorming: In light of our understanding of the causes of conflict how can we seek peace? Where can we begin looking for peace? How can we deal with the causes of conflict? Make a list of their responses.

Divide the class into small groups. Show the class the rest of the quotes. Ask them to discuss the quotes within their groups. To get them started give students a few questions to consider:

> What does kindness have to do with peace?
> How will mountains bearing grain bring peace? What does this say about the
> ultimate causes of conflict?
> What does wisdom have to do with peace?

Give students some time to discuss and compile a list of their responses.

Note: One thing you want the students to understand is that peace can come when people work and live together, and help one another.

Have each group share its responses, then talk about acts of kindness that could be the first small steps we could take toward peace. Remind the students that these small steps don't have to be the kind that you read about in the newspaper or hear about on the TV. They can be as simple as returning a grocery cart to its proper place; picking up someone else's litter; writing a thank you note to a teacher, a relative, or even a helpful new acquaintance; taking out the trash before you are told to do it; helping a sibling finish a task; or even playing a game with a sibling. These are just a few of the simple steps that can lead to a warmer, kinder world to live in.

Respect and Love—How Do They Go Together?

Prepare a handout, including the following quotes, and make copies for each student:

> Do not hate another person in your heart. (Leviticus 19:17)

> Love your neighbor as yourself. (Leviticus 19:18)

> The Holy One said to Israel:
> "My children, what do I seek from you? I seek no more than that
> you love one another and honor one another, and that you have awe
> and reverence for one another." (*Tanna D'vei Eliyahu Rabbah* 26:6)

Hillel taught: "Be a disciple of Aaron: loving peace and pursuing peace, loving your fellow creatures, and attracting them to the study of Torah." (*Pirkei Avot* 1:12)

Rabbi Eliezer said: "Let the honor of your fellow human being be as dear to you as your own." (*Pirkei Avot* 2:15)

The First Temple was destroyed because of the sins of idolatry, harlotry, and murder. The second, in spite of Torah studies, mitzvot, and deeds of love executed during its existence, fell because of groundless hatred. This teaches us that groundless hatred is a sin that weighs as heavily as idolatry, harlotry, and murder. (Babylonian Talmud *Yoma* 9b)

Rabbi Yochanan ben Torta said: "The destruction of the Second Temple came about because people loved money and hated one another." (*Tosefta, M'nachot* 13:22)

Distribute the handouts and ask the students to take turns reading these Jewish sources out loud. Discuss the contents, asking students:

What is the major theme?
How do you show love, caring, and concern?
What other words could be used besides "love"?
How would the word "respect" fit in with love?
How can you honor someone you do not like?
How can you respect someone you do not like?
If the Temple was destroyed because of hatred, what does that tell us about not liking someone? What can we do to change our attitude toward someone we don't like?

Let the students carry the discussion as much as possible, with you asking questions when necessary to move it along.

Now, ask students to choose a partner or divide them into pairs. Ask each person in the dyad to list three things that the two share in common and three things that are different about each other. Have them talk about the differences and similarities. How would this affect their potential for friendship or getting along with one another?

As a closure, ask each student to complete the following sentence with the first words that come to mind:

I can show love and respect to another person by _____ _____.

Invite those students who wish to share their completed sentences to do so.

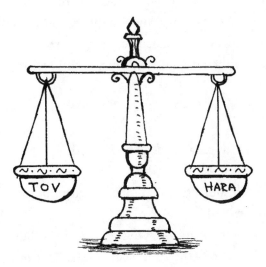

The *Yetzer Hatov* and the *Yetzer Hara*

According to tradition, each of us has both the inclination to be good *(yetzer hatov)* and the inclination to do evil *(yetzer hara)*. Our job is to keep them in balance. There was an activity I used to do years ago—just playing tug of war. I used a long, heavy rope and placed all the girls on one side and all the boys on the other side. Needless to say, the boys always seemed to win. We would talk about how unbalanced the teams were, then do the tug of war again. This time the boys and girls were evenly divided by size as well as by gender. Neither team could pull the other off balance, so there was never a winner the second time around. We then would talk about the *yetzer hatov* and *yetzer hara* and of how we need to keep them in balance.

Alternative
This activity is not quite as vigorous. Have the students look through the Book of Proverbs. Either have a Bible for each student, or choose a good number of proverbs yourself to use for this purpose, making copies for each student. As they read the proverbs, ask students to select those that would be good maxims to use in keeping the *yetzer hatov* and *yetzer hara* in balance.

Before class, go to your favorite camera store and ask the manager for as many of the empty film canisters as you can have. (These usually are thrown away.)

Have them available the day you do this activity, along with some small strips of paper. Once the students have chosen their proverbs to use, give them several film canisters and strips of paper. Tell students to write the proverbs on the strips of paper, one proverb per slip. Place the written proverb in a film canister—it now becomes our version of a fortune cookie. Place the filled canisters in a bag; have each student choose one, open it up, and read it. As closure, ask each student to design a logo that represents the balance between the *yetzer hatov* and *yetzer hara*, using the proverb as the theme. Allow students time to share their logos.

Travel Through Time

This is a little different approach to help students become more aware of our need to conserve and preserve the earth's natural resources. First, share with children quotes from Jewish sources that emphasize our responsibility to take care of the land, water, and air.

Divide the class into small groups. Give each group a different period of time to explore: the prehistoric era, the American colonial period, the 1800s, and so forth. The students are to become time travelers, with each group investigating its assigned period. Prepare your bulletin board to accept the students' work as they do their research, giving each group space to place its work. As they do their research, the students can consider the following questions:

What were the people like? What did they do for a living? Where did they live? and so on.
How did they use animals, or plants and trees?
How did they obtain light, heat, and water?
What existed then that does not exist now?
How were people during the given time period concerned about their environment? What, if anything, did they do about it?
What effect have their actions or inactions had on our world today?

Each group then writes a short report about its travels through time, illustrating it with drawings or pictures to emphasize the key points members would like to make. Post the findings on the bulletin board, and give each group time to make its presentation.

As a closure for this activity, have the class decide on a project that would save at least one item that they use everyday for future generations. For example, they could decide on a project for energy conservation such as using cars less or purchasing fuel efficient cars to protect the air.

Jewish Values in the News

In 1999, right after Hurricane Floyd hit North Carolina, I read a story about a man in the central United States who was dismayed at the plight of the people suffering from the hurricane's blast. This man was a truck driver. He went to his boss and asked if he could have the use of a truck and trailer during his time off. He explained what he wanted to do, and his boss gave him permission to use the truck and trailer. The man gathered together his friends and relatives, and they collected nonperishable foods, clothing, and bedding to fill the trailer, then took off for North Carolina—a ten-hour drive. In North Carolina he handed over all of what had been collected and then made the ten-hour drive back home. He gave the most precious gift of all to those in need: his time! The man was very generous.

Proverbs 22:9 says: "The generous person is blessed." The Talmud (*Nedarim* 38a) notes: "Rabbi Yosi, son of Rabbi Hanina said: 'The Torah was given only to Moses and his seed, for it is written, you [Moses] carve two tablets and I [God] will inscribe them' (Exodus 34:1). Just as the tablets are yours, so is the writing yours. But Moses in his generosity gave [the Torah] to Israel, and concerning this it is said, 'The generous person is blessed.'"

Share the story and the quotes with the students. Help them understand that our heritage considers them blessed. Then conduct a discussion, asking: What other kinds of acts of generosity can you think of? What difference does the generosity make? What kind of acts of generosity can children make? How about adults? Have students list things they can do to make a difference. Choose one that the class can do and make the appropriate plans to accomplish the deed.

Identify Acts of Kindness

Bring a week's worth of newspapers to class. Also prepare a list of five or ten Jewish values, with quotes to illustrate each value. Divide the class into small groups. Give out a newspaper to each group—several if necessary, and a copy of the list. The students' task is to find a picture or article that illustrates each value. They cut out the article/picture, then label it with the Jewish value that it represents. Have the groups share their pictures, then post the pictures on the bulletin board, grouping them by value.

Survival

This is a variation of a very old exercise I did more than twenty years ago. Divide the class into small learning groups. Prepare a box with sixteen to twenty index cards, each with one Jewish concept, value, or object written on it, such as Shabbat, God-idea, freedom, Torah, *siddur,* Hebrew, peace, Talmud, compassion, truth, holiness, menorah, *Kiddush* cup, candlesticks and candles, challah, and so forth. Place the cards in the box—have enough so each group can draw out five cards. Or, you can place five different index cards in an envelope and pass an envelope out to each group.

Next, tell the students that each group is going to imagine that the members are the leaders of a new Jewish community which is to be established on a deserted island. The students are to determine how they would use these ideas or items to ensure the survival of the Jewish people in this new location. Let their creative imagination go to work! When all the groups have finished, let students act out how they would ensure the Jews' survival.

After all the groups have made their presentations, discuss what was easy and what was difficult. What did they think was missing if the Jews were to survive?

Note: Only one group will have the card with "Torah" written on it, so that will really be the only group with nothing missing. The idea is that the Torah contains everything else on the list and it has been there for the Jews all these years. Hopefully, students will reach that conclusion on their own.

Television and Jewish Ethics

Give your students a homework assignment they won't complain about. Make use of something they enjoy doing—watching TV! This activity can be used as an introduction to famous Jewish people found within Jewish history or to the study of Jewish ethics and morals.

Identify, by previewing, the show or shows you want the kids to watch. Your best bets are family shows, like *The Nanny, Home Improvement, The Simpsons, Everybody Loves Raymond,* or *Gilmore Girls.* Don't limit yourself to network television; many suitable shows are in syndication or on cable. Prepare a questionnaire that includes at the top the name of the show and the station and time it is on. Then list the questions you want the students to answer after they have watched the show. The questions should reflect the nature of the show and the point you want to make. Here are three sample questionnaires:

Questionnaire 1

1. Which character would you consider to be a hero or heroine? Explain.

2. What personal qualities make this character a hero or heroine?
3. What problems did this character encounter?
4. How did he or she overcome these problems?
5. In what way was this character a positive role model?
6. What did this character learn from his or her actions?
7. How does this character fit your idea of a hero or heroine?
8. In what way does an everyday hero or heroine differ from a fictional one?
9. What responsibility does a hero or heroine have to serve as a role model?
10. What are the different qualities a hero or heroine should have?

Questionnaire 2

1. Of what was the show making fun?
2. Make a list of the Ten Commandments broken in the show.
3. Define the personal qualities of the main character of this show.
4. In what way was any character in the show a positive or negative role model? Explain.
5. What negative or positive message did you get out of the show?
6. What stereotypes were portrayed during the show?
7. What would a person learn from watching this show on a regular basis?

Questionnaire 3

1. How does your favorite character on this show talk, act, and make decisions?
2. What is Jewish about this person?
3. How does he or she arrive at decisions?
4. What Jewish value is involved in his or her decision making?
5. Who or what influences the character?
6. How are the women and racial minorities portrayed?
7. How are they treated? How would you treat them?
8. What adjectives describe the women? The men?

The completed questionnaires become the basis for a class discussion. Look for opportunities, based on students' comments, not only to identify Jewish values, but to bring to the forefront any negative aspects of the show. As a follow-up activity, encourage the students to write letters to the producer either objecting to questionable content or praising positive presentations.

That's Not Fair!

Regardless of age, almost every person makes this statement when he or she thinks his or her rights have been violated. A discussion about fairness is an excellent starting place for the study of Jewish ethics and values.

Ask the students: "What do you mean when you say something is not fair?" Make a list of students' responses. Initially you may get such answers as "My sister gets more allowance than I do" or "My brother stays up later than I do." Keep after the students, though, and you will begin to get other statements, like, "I saw a friend cheating on a test," "My friend took a CD and didn't pay for it," or "I was accused of cheating—but my friend, who also cheated, wasn't."

Choose a scenario, either hypothetical or from the list students have generated. It should reflect the proper level of understanding of the students. This time use the question, "What would you do?" Offer students a number of options from which to choose, including a final option of "Would you do something else?" Students can consider the following when deciding what they would do:

Would I want the same solution applied to me if the roles were reversed?
Would I want everyone to employ this solution or follow this example?
Is this rule being applied similarly to other individuals or groups?
How would I view the situation if I did not have a personal interest in it?
What solution would be the best for the greatest number?

Be sure to use materials from Jewish sources to help understand the "fairness" of Jewish ethics.

PRESERVING OUR WORLD

We are told that people are the guardians, rather than the masters, of God's creations. God created the world and made human beings "partners in the world of creation" (Babylonian Talmud *Shabbat* 10a). As guardians and custodians of the world, we are obliged to preserve nature and to guard it against destruction or damage. What follows are a few activities that can show our students how our ancestors were "ahead of their time" when it came to environmental issues. Ecology is nothing new!

Find the Biblical Sources

Either have Bibles for the students, or prepare a sheet containing the texts of Leviticus 19:23–25 and 25:2–7, and Deuteronomy 8:1, 7–10, and 20:19–20.

Students are to read these portions, then talk about the characteristics of the land the Israelites are about to enter. In small groups, students are to make a list describing what the Israelites will need to do to protect the land and the trees, and what benefits the people will derive from the land and the trees. Upon completion, groups share their lists and make one composite list on the board.

The Beauty of God's Creation

Prepare a sheet with the following, taken from Psalm 104:

> You spread out the heavens like a tent of cloth.
> You make the winds Your messengers.
> You make the grass grow for the cattle and herbage for our labor;
> that we may get food out of the earth.
> The trees of the Eternal drink their fill.
> There is the sea, vast and wide, with its creatures beyond number,
> living things, small and great.
> How many are the things You have made O Eternal.
> You have made them with wisdom; the earth is full of your creatures.
> May the glory of the Eternal endure forever.

The students are to choose one of the lines from the psalm and explain how human beings are destroying that aspect of nature. Let them create any one of the following to explain:

Poster-size drawing
Poem
Musical parody or rap
Newspaper or magazine article
News broadcast

Upon completion, students share their work with the class.

Do Something About It!

Read aloud the following text, or copy and hand it out to the students:

> When a fruit bearing tree is chopped down, a voice is heard from one end of the world to the other, but it is not audible (to the human ear). (*Pirkei d'R. Eliezer* 34)

> Rabbi Yehuda said: "One who goes out in the month of Nisan (in the spring) and sees trees coming into leaf says, 'Blessed be Adonai, Who has made the world so that it lacks nothing, and created good creatures, and good trees, for the pleasure of people.'" (Babylonian Talmud *B'rachot* 43b)

> Think upon this, and do not corrupt and desolate My world. For if you corrupt or desolate it, there is no one to set it right after you. (*Kohelet Rabbah* 7:28)

After reading, do some brainstorming, making a list of all the ways we are destroying the world. Talk about what effect this destruction has on us and what responsibility we have to preserve the world. From the list that the class created, choose one issue that the class would like to address. What action could the class take to make a difference? Help students prepare an outline of a plan of action, then proceed with the project!

Earth Day: Protecting Our Environment

Talk about how we must take care of our environment. Point out that it is a Jewish responsibility, as well as an obligation for everyone in our society. Prepare a number of "What would you do if . . ." statements for the students to consider. Here are a few to get you started.

What would you do if . . .

- You are riding in the car with your parents. Your father is munching on a candy bar, and when he finishes he tosses the candy wrapper out the window.
- You are babysitting, and the child you are watching is brushing his teeth. He insists on keeping the water faucet on the whole time.

- You are visiting your aunt, and when she finishes reading the newspaper she tosses it into the garbage can.

When you have finished, have the students make a list of all the things they can do to help preserve the earth and its environment.

Caring Communities

Many congregations across the country have "caring community" committees. Their purpose, in most instances, is to assist those in need, as we have been commanded. Our Jewish sources are full of admonitions to care for the sick and the elderly, leave the corner of the field, and so on. What follows are a few quotes from the Bible, Talmud, and midrash—just a sample of what is found in our Jewish tradition. There are a variety of ways these can be used. All of them have the possibility of leading to some action on the part of your class: "We shall listen and we shall do."

Some of the many quotations from the Bible (look them up!) include Leviticus 19:9, 14, 33–34 and 23:22; Deuteronomy 15:7–8 and 10:17–19; Psalms 72:2, 4 and 82:3; Isaiah 1:17 and 54:13; Zechariah 8:5; Proverbs 3:3, 14:31, and 15:1; Jeremiah 31:8–9; and Ecclesiastes 9:6. In addition, try some of the following:

Pirkei Avot 1:2—The world stands on Torah, worship, and deeds of loving-kindness.

Pirkei Avot 1:5—Let your house be open; let the poor be members of your household.

N'darim 81a—Do not neglect the children of the poor, for from them will go forth the law.

Avodah Zarah 17b—Whoever busies himself in the study of the Law alone, without engaging in acts of loving-kindness, is like one who recognizes no God.

Whichever quote you use, place it on the board and read it aloud. Also have prepared a list of questions to use as a guide for discussion so the students understand what it means. Suppose you choose Deuteronomy 15:7–8:

If, however, there is a needy person among you, one of your kinsmen in any of your settlements in the land that the Lord your God is giving you, do not harden your heart and shut your hand against your needy kinsman. Rather, you must open your hand and lend him sufficient for whatever he needs.

Your list of questions could look something like this:

Who do you think is a needy person? (Brainstorm, making a list of those whom students consider to be needy.)
What does it mean to harden your heart?
Who else can you think of who "hardened his heart"? *[Pharaoh]*
What is the difference between a shut hand and an open hand?
How can you open your hand to help the needy?

After you are sure the students understand the meaning of the quote, choose one of the following activities for the students to do, or give them a choice:

1. Divide the class into small groups. Have each group choose a different quote; or, give a different quote to each group. Each group is to create a poster emphasizing the meaning and importance of the message of the quote.
2. Bring at least a week's supply of local newspapers to class. Divide the class into small groups. Give each group several days of newspapers. Members are to find articles that exemplify the meaning of the quote. If a group cannot find an article, the group is to write its own news report, giving what members think is an example of the quote.
3. Divide the class into small groups. Each group is to create a three-minute skit that gives an example of the meaning of the quote.

Slow to Anger

We need to spend some time with our students discussing the importance of this value. Give students a chance to see what makes people angry and hurt—then maybe students will curb their own actions, and also learn to control their own emotions when others do not know better. There are a number of Jewish sources that illustrate our need to control our anger. Probably the most prominent one is Numbers 20, which describes how Moses loses his temper at the Waters of Meribah. The Israelites are complaining about the lack of water and proper food. God tells Moses to speak to the rock to get water from it, but Moses is so angry, he strikes it. Water still comes from the rock, but because of his loss of self-control, Moses loses the opportunity to enter the promised Land of Israel. In

Proverbs 14:17 we read: "Slowness to anger results in much understanding; impatience brings about folly." Also, there is a marvelous midrash in the Talmud (*Shabbat* 31a) that tells the story of the man who is determined to make Hillel angry. The man keeps disturbing Hillel by asking foolish questions, even betting someone 400 *zuz* that he can make Hillel angry. Of course, the ending of the story shows the foolish man losing his money. Hillel tells him, "Better you should lose your money then I lose my self-control."

Begin a lesson by sharing some of these Jewish sources about controlling one's anger. Then discuss with the students what makes them angry or hurt. This list can include such things as teasing, name calling, gossip, and so on. Do some brainstorming and make a list on the board.

Divide the class into two groups. Have one group choose one of the situations from the list. Give the group a few minutes to plan a presentation that shows how members would react to the situation. The other group watches; when the presentation is completed, members discuss the first group's interpretation and how observers responded. They are to consider such questions as:

What effort did students make to control their temper?
What was accomplished by controlling their temper?
What would they do differently?

Then, give the second group a turn to choose a situation and prepare a presentation. The first group watches and discusses members' reaction.

A closure for this activity could be for the students to come up with ways they can teach others to be "slow to anger." One of the ways would be for the kids to learn that their teasing and name calling *are* hurtful to others. Divide the class into small groups and ask the groups to develop some ideas and guidelines that would help them and others remember not to be hurtful to others. Allow each group to share its ideas and guidelines with the whole class, and come up with a composite list. Each group can create an attractive poster to convey its message. Place these posters around the school.

Coat of Arms or Family Crest

This is an old values clarification exercise. Even though some people say values clarification is more or less passé, I think it is an activity that still has some worth. The difference is that here, students' choices will be based on what they have studied and at this time in their lives they want to make some decisions. Even though some decisions will change as students get older, this is a beginning.

Share the quote "You shall be holy, for I, the Eternal your God, am holy" (Leviticus 19:2), brainstorming with students a list of what they consider it means to be holy. Leave the list up, then give students copies of the text from Exodus 34:6–7:

> The Lord passed before him [Moses] and proclaimed: "Adonai! Adonai! A God compassionate and gracious, slow to anger, abounding in kindness and faithfulness, extending kindness to the thousandth generation, forgiving iniquity, transgression, and sin; yet God does not remit all punishment, but visits the iniquity of the parents upon children and children's children, upon the third and fourth generations."

Divide the class into small groups. Each group is to make a list of the character traits of God that it finds in the passage from Exodus. Don't stop there, though. Give students some *siddurim*, and let's see how many other character traits or attributes of God they can find to add to their lists. Each group shares its finds. Compile a composite list on the board.

Each group is to choose those character traits of God that members think are the most important to them. They will need to reach consensus, rank-ordering the list as to the ten most important. By consensus, I mean each person in the group must feel comfortable with the choices—each person just might have to give in a little.

Once they have made their choices, students are to design a Jewish values crest, placing the most important value in the center and the rest around it. The group will need to create symbols that represent the different character traits and then identify them as part of its crest. Once completed, the groups share their works of art and place them around the room.

An extension of this activity would be for each student to create his or her own personal coat of arms based on their individual choices of character traits. Or, have children work at home with parents (and siblings) to design a family coat of arms, which students share in class the following week.

Drama in the Classroom

Using the texts of Leviticus 19:2 and Exodus 34:6–7 (see the previous activity), study and discuss the verses. Divide the class into small groups. Give each group two or three of God's character traits and the same number of "negative" traits (these are not God's, but are faults prevalent in our society). Each group is to create a play. The play is to be a dialogue among the different values as they try to define themselves and their importance. The negative traits are to be included as devil's advocates to the positive values. Give groups time to create and then time to practice. Each group presents its play to the whole class.

A closure for any of these activities: We are told to be holy for God is holy. One of the ways we can achieve holiness, or come close to it, would be to demonstrate our care and concern for others. Have the class choose a charity or cause that reflects what students consider to be the most important character trait of God. Students then design a logo for that charity or cause, develop an advertising campaign, and design posters. Contact the charity or cause to share what your class has done. Identify a way the class can actually do something that helps the charity or cause: raising money, collecting needed supplies, and so on. Just go for it! This kind of activity will not only place the values in perspective, but will make them come alive and seem more real to the students.

A Potpourri of Ideas

Internet Scavenger Hunt

This special event comes from Diane Blum and Mindy Eisen of Temple Emanuel, Beaumont, Texas.

Determine which students have at-home computers with Internet access. Obtain permission from the religious school and from parents to have session at students' homes. Break students up into teams of three. Each team will work at one team member's home to answer a list of twenty or so questions. All the answers will be found on the Internet. (*Note:* Be sure to arrange for a parent to supervise students the entire time they are on the Internet.) The questions can be linked to your unit of study, or they can range over a wide number of subjects. Some of the questions created by Diane Blum and Mindy Eisen were:

1. Find a Jewish-themed cartoon. Either print it or get the parent supervisor to verify the hit.
2. Locate a picture of the Western Wall in Jerusalem.
3. Find the address and URL of the Confederascao Israelita do Brasil, in Brazil.
4. Name one country in the New World with fewer than one hundred Jews.
5. How many prophets does the Torah recognize?

6. What are the names of the female prophets?

7. What is the address of the Israeli Embassy in Washington, D.C.? Sign the guest book and get the adult in charge to verify it.

8. List the stage names, real names, and birth dates of all the Marx Brothers.

9. What's the Yiddish word for "nervous energy"?

10. How many extra-base hits did Hank Greenberg get in 1940?

Arrange for everyone to meet at the school at a certain time. Serve refreshments and go over the answers. Don't forget to give a prize to the team that gets the most questions right.

Pictures Make a Book

Pictures taken with a camera, that is.

First, the class will need to identify the theme of the book. The picture book could be based on your unit of study. Or, the kids could choose one concept from their studies from which to build their book, for example, caring for the widow and orphan. Environmental issues lend themselves very well to this idea, too—conservation of water; saving trees because of all they do for us, and so on. Alternatively, you could have several themes and divide your class into small groups. Have each group choose a theme, and give each group a disposable camera.

With the class, prepare a general outline for what is to be included in the book. Post this outline in plain view so groups can easily refer to it. Each group prepares a more specific outline, based on its topic, of what pictures need to be taken to tell the story. Students can first write a theme-related short story, then take the pictures to go with the story. Or, students can take the pictures they want, then write the story to go with the pictures. Choose one of these two ways to do this activity for the whole class.

Give the students time to take their pictures and have them developed. A word of caution: tell the students to take several pictures of the same subject from different angles with different lighting to be sure they get the effect they want. When they have their pictures, supply students with enough paper to put together their book. Bind the book together with brass fasteners. Allow students to share their books with one another.

A few potential themes for picture books:

Tzedakah
Celebrating the Sabbath from beginning to end

Jewish community guide book
Preparing for Passover
The Ten Commandments

Let's Talk

Pick a card and let's talk! This is a good way to open discussion and get everyone talking. All you have to do is prepare a deck of cards, each containing an interesting fact based on your unit of study and an open-ended question relating to the fact that encourages the students to express their thoughts, ideas, and opinions. You can also make these cards out of 3 x 5 index cards, then laminate or cover with clear contact paper. Make as many as needed for each student to choose two or three cards.

Have a student pick a card, read the fact out loud, and ask the question. Encourage each child to respond to the question or offer an opinion. Be sure students are accepting of one another's responses since these might be personal opinions or ideas.

Fan Letter

Ask each student to write a fan letter to a famous Jewish person from your unit of study. In his or her letter, the student can explain why he or she admires and respects this person.

Students Become Detectives

Write a paragraph that summarizes the lesson, but intentionally make five or six mistakes in your summary. Use triple-space so the students have room to write the correct information. The students are to find the mistakes, circle them, and write the correct answers in the space provided.

True/False Statements: Prepare at least ten true or false statements. When a student thinks an answer is "false," he or she must write why it is a false answer.

Making Lists

Challenge the students to make lists related to your unit of study. Just to give you some ideas, they could make lists of any one of the following:

What they do to celebrate Shabbat
What they would like to tell their great-grandparents

The foods they eat during Pesach
What they would say to David Ben-Gurion on meeting him
What is important to them about Israel

Once their lists are completed, students can share them with the class.

Backward Crossword Puzzle

Prepare crossword puzzles that are already filled in. Ask the students to come up with the clues for each word. You could even make up several different crossword puzzles; divide the class into small groups, giving each group a different puzzle. The groups come up with the clues, then white-out the answers in the original crossword puzzle to give to other groups to complete.

Bumper Stickers

Instead of the usual poster, mural, or collage, give this a try. Have your students design bumper stickers with statements that reflect their feelings about a certain Jewish value or issue. Give them art materials: construction paper, colored markers, and so forth. Display the bumper stickers around the room. You can even make them realistic by using sticky-back paper cut into strips, or brightly colored contact paper with no designs—then they really could be used as bumper stickers!

Discovering the Facts

Prepare your bulletin board or wall space for a unit mural that the students can use. Explain to the students that as they discover new information, they are to write the information on an index card and place it on the board. If you are using a bulletin board, have thumbtacks available; if students will be creating a mural, have removable tape available. This will allow the students to easily move the information cards around so related facts are in close proximity.

Caution the kids to always check what facts are already in place to avoid duplication. To complete the project, after all the facts are in place, have the students add pictures, symbols, and any other decorations that will enhance the presentation. By the end of the unit of study, your class will have a very attractive and informative presentation.

Helpful Hints

Working with Students

MOTIVATING YOUR STUDENTS

What works to keep your students' attention? Research shows you've got fifteen seconds before you lose them; but if you use some of these proven techniques, you can keep students motivated:

1. *Make your lessons fast paced.* Every time your lesson drags you risk losing your students' attention.
2. *Give students a chance to work in small groups.* Small groups encourage students to participate in discussions, help them work out problems, and enable students to learn more.
3. *Make lessons active.* Students learn by doing. So let them become actively involved.
4. *Tightly focus your lessons.* Pick a few objectives to concentrate on. Students will do more thinking for a few objectives then they will for a broad, unfocused lesson.
5. *Be consistent.* Establish patterns for how you discipline, organize your lessons, and expect students to behave—then stick to them!

6. *Help your students understand why what they're learning is important.* At the very beginning of a lesson, show how the subject matter connects to real life and why it is important to them.

7. *Give students a stake in their learning.* Students learn more if they have a vested interest in the subject. Let them make choices, determine results, identify resources, even experiment.

8. *Go deeper with topics and themes.* For example, if your topic is a law from the Torah, let them dig deeper to find different explanations of the law and its meaning, how the law affects them today, and how appropriate it is for today's life.

Scramble It Up

Place on the board well-scrambled letters of a word or phrase that has to do with the lesson. As the students arrive, they can race to see who can unscramble the letters first. This will give them insight as to the lesson for the day, and it will also keep them occupied during the first few minutes of class.

"I Made a Difference"

When students have done something nice, performed a mitzvah, or given of themselves, be sure to let them know that they have made a difference.

Make up brightly colored ribbons which you have printed with "I made a difference." Pin these on students who have made a difference. Or, you can have badges made which say the same thing.

More About Motivation

Recent research has told us that students want work that stimulates their curiosity, permits them to express their creativity, and fosters positive relationships with others. Students are driven by four goals, each of which satisfies a particular human need:

Success: the need to master a skill
Curiosity: the need for understanding
Originality: the need for self expression (creativity)
Relationships: the need for involvement with others

Students want and need work that enables them to demonstrate and improve their sense of worth. Before we can use success to motivate our students we must meet three conditions:

1. We must clearly articulate the criteria for success and provide clear, immediate, and constructive feedback.
2. We must show students that the skills they need to be successful are within their grasp by clearly modeling these skills.
3. We must help them see that success is a valuable aspect of their personalities.

Suppose the class is reading a text, and you have asked your students to find the central theme. Work with them to "find" that main idea, which is usually a sentence stating the position on the topic.

Keep in mind the use of brainstorming. This helps students to think creatively. Model the process of brainstorming, demonstrating that no idea is unworthy of consideration.

Arouse students' curiosity. Students desire work that stimulates their curiosity. We can be certain that our curriculum does so by making sure it contains two defining characteristics: a topic that relates to the student's personal lives, and information about the topic that is fragmentary or contradictory. It is said that the lack of organization in a body of information compels us to understand it further. By providing a "mystery," we present the class with a problem. Suppose you ask the class: What was the cause for the establishment of the State of Israel? Students then work together tracing the steps in Jewish history to arrive at an explanation.

Make it personal. When it comes to what is personal in the students' lives, you must determine what issues they are confronting today. How can these issues be connected with the curriculum? For example, in studying the Six-Day War, students learn that the Israelis reacted "before" the Arabs could attack them. This can lead to a discussion guide on whether it is proper to react before an action takes place. What kind of action could be taken? When? Choose issues that are of concern to the students and identify these issues prior to any lessons.

Encourage originality and creativity. Encouraging self-expression in your students can be accomplished in a number of ways:

- *Connect creative projects to student's personal ideas and concerns.* For example, suppose you are studying holiday celebrations in the home. Ask the students to create a religious object they can use at home during a holiday. Let them use their imagination to create this item; do not tell them what to create!

- *Expand what counts as an audience:* We are used to audiences made up of many people, but consider an audience of one! For example, a wonderful activity would be for your students to become involved with the elderly, either in a nursing home or in your own congregation. Assign one elderly person to each child. The student's task would be to work with this person and create his or her "autobiography."

- *Consider giving students more choices:* Once you assign students a task, let them choose how to make their presentations. There are a lot of options: art, drama, music, creative writing, videography, photography. Such opportunities allow students to make the most of their different learning styles and intelligences.

Create relationships. Often, when I introduce an activity, I have students form small groups within the class. Today these are called cooperative learning groups. Such groups allow students to develop positive relations with their peers. Keep rotating the groups and their individual assignments to be sure everyone has an opportunity to work with each member of the class.

Lesson Planning

WHY PLAN LESSONS?

Even though you might be the most experienced teacher, it never hurts to remind yourself of the objectives of a lesson. In an article in the winter 1998 issue of the *CCAR Journal,* "Toward a Coherent Curriculum for Our Religious Schools," Rabbi Sam Joseph said:

> What do we want our students to do with the knowledge derived from studying Bible, holidays, life cycles, and so on? Can our students see the value of what they are studying? All that occurs in the religious school, from the moment they enter Kindergarten until they graduate, should build toward meaning. The classes they attend are not in isolation, factoid of history here, Bible there. The student's schooling must lead somewhere, toward living out the vision of the congregation.

The vision of your class should be based on the idea that your students will obtain knowledge necessary to live meaningful Jewish lives. So keep the following in mind when planning your lesson:

1. Think about what engages your students' attention. Try your best to relate what you are teaching to their interests.
2. Get the students emotionally involved by giving them choices. For example, when giving a reading assignment, offer them eight to ten activities to choose from.
3. Let the children know that you enjoy what you are doing and that you are thrilled to be transmitting our Jewish heritage.
4. Make the pages of history come alive! Role playing is one way. The students can also "become" a person in that period of time. For a unit on the Exodus from Egypt, some students could write a news article about how it felt to cross the Sea of Reeds; others could express their impressions in a mural, while those who are musically inclined could write a parody that describes the experience.
5. Ask yourself: If I were the student, would I like this lesson? Would it get me excited? Would it make me think? If you can answer "yes" to *all* the questions, continue. If not, go back to the drawing board. If you are excited about the lesson, the kids will sense it and become involved.
6. Investigate the possibility of using video or audio tapes with your lesson. They can often set the mood or enhance the subject.
7. Get the students to share their feelings. If you share your feelings, children often respond in kind.

WHEN PLANNING LESSONS . . .

Identify your objectives. Why are you teaching this lesson? What are the most important ideas to be gained from this lesson? How does it fit into the entire curriculum?

Teach the essentials. What is of major importance? What specific information are the students to obtain from this lesson? What is essential for the student's understanding of the lesson? What other sources or references can be used for additional information? How can the unit of study be most effectively organized?

Motivate students. Why should students study this material? How can you show the relationship or connection to their present day needs, interests, and experiences? How can it be compared to something with which the students are familiar? What questions can I ask them, or what can I show them that will arouse their interest? What kind of activities can I use that will catch the attention of each and every student, regardless of learning style?

Finding Out What the Kids Want to Know

This can be used any time you begin a new unit of study. Prepare a poster that names the unit of study you are about to begin. Point it out to the students and encourage them to think for a minute about any questions they may have on the subject. Let students come up to the poster and write their questions directly on the poster. Then, as you go though this unit of study, incorporate their questions into your lessons. As a student's question is discussed or answered, have that child check that question off on the poster. This way, the students will feel that they were involved in determining their studies.

For New Teachers

If you are a new teacher, consider the following:

1. *Know your material.* Read the complete text your students will be using. Become familiar with its contents. While reading, identify major concepts you think are important to cover, making notes as needed.
2. *Use other resources.* Using a recommendation by your principal or the teacher's guide to your textbook, choose one other resource book on the same subject matter. Read it! This will give you a much wider perspective on the subject matter. Be sure to make notes about major concepts and ideas you gain from reading this additional material.

3. *When reading the subject matter, consider the following:*

Who are my students?

What do I know about my students?

What are the key concepts?

How will the topics connect with students' concerns, interests, and needs?

What key concepts studied in class will contribute to their lives?

How would the topic help students to grow?

4. *Choose objectives.* What are the aims of your lesson? What will the students learn, be able to do, or achieve from this lesson? What changes in their behavior will be accomplished? Educational goals are skills, understanding, and knowledge, whereas concrete goals are attitude and observable changes in behavior. Instructional objectives are not goals. They are brief, clear statements that describe what kind of performance the student is expected to demonstrate when the lesson is completed. They are sometimes called intended outcomes, learning outcomes, or desired results.

Instructional objectives are small steps toward the larger goal. They are very specific and reflect the performance of students once they have mastered the subject matter. The following words reflect specific performance and can help you when you write your instructional objectives while preparing your lesson plan: list, define, explain, justify, summarize, write, diagram, create, relate, organize, tell, contrast, defend, distinguish, solve, give examples, demonstrate, interpret, describe, identify, differentiate, illustrate, and compare.

Here are some sample instructional objectives:

Students will be able to explain their view of God in poetry, song, or essay.

Students will be able identify the symbols of Rosh Hashanah and Yom Kippur.

Students will be able to create a kibbutz out of blocks.

Students will be able to list the various ways they identify as Jews.

Students will be able to describe life in a concentration camp.

Student will be able to define the meaning of *tzedakah*.

Students will be able to tell the story of Purim and explain how we celebrate it.

5. *Consider resources for students.* What readings will you use? Who in the congregation could add substance to the lesson or act as resources? What pictures, videos, or movies would enrich the lesson?

6. *When selecting classroom activities, ask yourself:*

What teaching methods would be most appropriate?

What senses can the lesson appeal to?

How can the lesson appeal to different levels of intelligence, learning abilities, and styles?

How can the lesson allow for student movement?

How can I be sure the students are actively involved in doing things?

How can I relate the lesson to students' lives?

What kind of eye-opening activity can I begin the lesson with to motivate the students?

What questions will stimulate thought?

What group organization would be the most appropriate?

What materials will I need?

7. *Think about how to use art in the classroom.*

Don't overlook the use of art in the classroom! I don't mean just drawing a picture—yes, that's art, but not the kind I am talking about. Art is a means of expressing oneself. I recently read an article about visual arts in which the author used prehistoric cave paintings as an example of how people have communicated using the visual arts. So, let's think about art as a means of communication. Keep in mind that each student does not have to be a great artist, but all students can express themselves through art. Whether stick figures (and some of the cave drawings were just that) or blocks of colors, art is an expression of what students are thinking or feeling. Depending on your unit of study, art can be used to let the students reach another level of thought about the matter.

8. *Think about long-term results.* Consider what actions the students might be able to take as a result of the lesson. What actions will bring the lesson into their own lives? How can the students utilize what they have learned as a result of the lesson? Say you have just done a lesson on *tzedakah,* using different quotes from the Bible, which, among other things, calls on us to leave the corner of our fields for the poor and the orphans. This is a great opportunity for kids to put together a *tzedakah* project, for example,  gathering food for a food bank and reaching out to the entire congregation to take part.

Long-term Plans

These classroom projects take some planning and can run the entire year. For example, if you are teaching a portion of Jewish history, you can incorporate into your lessons some arts and craft projects, drama, and music to provide some variety to your lessons. Once you thoroughly know the material you are going to teach, do some brainstorming—with other teachers, if possible—for different ideas that could be used. Creating a museum in your classroom would give you a number of opportunities for arts and crafts. Develop the format for a play that the students could write and produce based on a portion of the subject matter; and identify music and songs from the period of history being studied which could be used in the classroom for additional information about that period of time.

Some Final Suggestions

Whether you are the head of a school or a new teacher, it is never too late to try some of these ideas:

1. Choose a buddy or ask an experienced teacher to work with you. Share ideas, discuss problems, and lend a supportive ear.
2. If you are a seasoned teacher, introduce yourself to the new teachers. Let them know you are available to answer questions and talk.
3. If you are a new teacher, ask a seasoned teacher how he or she handled a problem. It's a great way to break the ice.
4. On a regular basis, have grade-level or teacher meetings for the entire school to get to really know one another, brainstorm and share creative teaching ideas, or have study sessions.
5. Use your education director as a resource for ideas.

Families—Be Sensitive

A gentle tip when working on study units about families. In this day and age you need to be sensitive to the different types of families that abound. According to current research, a complete definition would include more than thirty different family types. Some of these would include single parent households, stepfamilies, adoptive families, extended families, and blended families. When using pictures of family units display pictures of *all* types of families. Do not group them in specific areas! Just place them randomly around the room. When doing family trees or family time lines, word them so they include all kinds of families.

Keep in mind that a student's "family" could be made up not just of relatives but other beloved people as well. You might even consider having students investigate the different kind of family units there are. Invite representatives from different families to talk about the challenges, difficulties, and rewards of their kind of family unit.

Regardless of the kind of family unit, divide the class into small groups. Each group is to make up a list of the challenges that members face, describing how these challenges are handled and how the children help. These can be compared to the families in your unit of study.

As closure, have students make a collage of "Family Love." Keep in mind "family love" can describe any group of people who love and care for one another. Remind students that family love means more than expressing affections. It also includes such things as setting limits, teaching, listening, and even disciplining. The collage can be made up from pictures found in magazines, newspapers, and advertisements, or students can draw the pictures they want in their collage.

HOW DO YOU BEGIN YOUR LESSONS?

Attention Grabbers

More commonly known as set inductions, these are ways to quickly get your students' attention. They set the mood for your lesson and establish an atmosphere of excitement and interest.

Set inductions are nothing new—they are as old as the Talmud. Before they began teaching, rabbis used to say something humorous to their scholars in order to amuse them (see Babylonian Talmud *P'sahim* 117a). Good teachers know they need to get their students' attention and make them feel comfortable.

Before creating your set inductions, consider that a good set induction grabs the students' attention, recalls prior knowledge, capitalizes on something they already know, zooms them right into the content, and mentally prepares them to learn. Here are a few examples:

- It was a lesson about lost articles, and their first Mishnah lesson, but the students didn't know that. As they came in and hung up their jackets, someone spotted some money lying on the floor. Students asked one another: "Do you know who dropped this?" "Finders, keepers?" "What should we do with it?" They were still asking questions as they took their seats, and then the teacher began her first lesson from the Mishnah, on lost articles.

154

- One teacher is teaching Shabbat. Every week when the students come in to the classroom, they find a beautifully set Shabbat table and Shabbat music playing in the background. The table, music, and ritual items set the tone for the instruction.
- Use fancy or crazy titles for lessons. One rabbi teaches midrash, and each week he places on the chalkboard the title for the lesson of the day. Examples include "Oops" (for a lesson on mistakes), "Eeny, Meeny, Miny, Mo" (for a lesson involving varieties of food); and "Last but Not Least" (for a lesson on which blessings to recite after some of the seven species). The students, who are used to looking for the new lesson title on the board, start asking questions as soon as they walk into the room.
- Puzzles, puzzles, everywhere. Using blank puzzles available from art and school supply stores, prepare a puzzle so that each student receives a piece. The puzzle should have something to do with the lesson: either a quote, a question, or a picture. Give one piece to each student as they arrive and they can begin to put together the puzzle, leading into the lesson.
- Don't be afraid to do something ridiculous to wake up your class and bring it to life. You will catch the students' attention, and you might even make them laugh. If learning is fun, they will remember what you teach.

As an example, try this some time: Climb up on top of your desk and announce in a booming voice (ignoring the kids with their mouths hanging open): "My dear friends, we are gathered together to witness the first meeting of Moses, Aaron, and Pharaoh." Point to one student and call him or her Moses, call another student Aaron, and call a third student Pharaoh. Then, let the role playing begin. After a few minutes, assign other kids the roles. (Don't forget to include the girls in the role playing.) Discuss how well Moses and Aaron did. This can lead to a discussion about the use of diplomacy in today's world, thereby bringing current events into the lesson. You began the lesson with a "bang" and caught students' attention, besides catching them totally unaware. They didn't have time to complain.

This same approach can work with any subject matter. Imagine having the class attend the wedding of Jacob and Leah! Or, visualize when the angels told Abraham and Sarah that at the age of ninety she would have a child!

Opening Day Activities

THE FIRST DAY OF SCHOOL

A good way to start the school year is by sending welcome letters to your students, giving them a brief idea of what will take place this year. Use the letter to introduce yourself. You can also ask students to bring something special to school the first day to introduce themselves to you. To make your letter extra special, include a nicely decorated certificate headed "Religious School Memories." Ask parents and children to write or sketch a special religious school memory from their past. Have the students bring these to the first day of school to share with the rest of the class. Decorate the bulletin board with the students' "memories."

Decorate the Classroom

You could have the door to your classroom decorated as a welcome to the kids. This is especially well suited for younger students. Choose a theme and cut out related Jewish symbols. Place each child's name on one and decorate your door with the personalized symbols.

Student Invitations

If you are teaching a group of children who are coming to school for the first time, send them invitations to the first day of school. Make it attractive and interesting. Include the room number, your name, and a little something about you. Ask them to bring something special to school that will tell everyone who they are.

Introducing Yourself

Gather together some pictures of yourself that span your life. Include those special people in your life. If you have a pet, be sure to include it as well. Mount each picture on an 8½ x 11 sheet of paper and write a short, easy-to-read caption underneath. Place each page into a plastic sheet protector. Arrange the sheets in a proper sequence and place them in a binder. Decorate the cover and add a title. Use this "autobiography" to introduce yourself to your students. Because you are sharing something of yourself, the children will likely be more eager to share something of themselves in return.

Making the Classroom Attractive

Prepare some large name tags. Cut out symbols from brightly colored paper or card stock. Place each child's name on a tag, then laminate or cover with clear contact paper. Tape a name tag to each student's desk. If you want, allow students to first decorate the tags. To get your class off to an especially "sweet" start, attach a piece of candy to each name tag.

Display Jewish posters around the room. The Jewish National Fund, El Al Airlines, and your regional Israeli consulate are all good sources. You can even create your own using magazine photos and old calendar pages.

Identify quotes from Jewish texts and place them attractively on brightly colored oak tag. Laminate or cover with clear contact paper and hang those up in the room, too.

Class Motto

Ask each student to write on colorful strips of paper his or her name, a self-description of his or her personality, and what he or she likes about religious school. Place all the strips in a box or bag. Draw three or four strips out of the bag and read the names aloud. These students will form a group. Continue until all the students have been grouped.

Tell groups to read one another's strips and talk about how they can work together. Then ask each group to design a class motto on construction paper. Have each group share its motto. The students can either choose the motto they like best and adopt it as their class motto, or they can decide to use all the mottos, one at a time, rotating periodically.

GETTING-TO-KNOW-YOU ACTIVITIES

Wooden Name Tags

Purchase wooden beads from a hobby or craft store. Select the size you want to use, but be sure to choose beads with holes in the center. If available, square beads are easier to work with. For each child, place one letter of his or her name around the bead, using a permanent felt-tip marker, until you have spelled out the child's name. I use a thin twine to hold the "names," but satin cord, wool, or even string are fine. Make one wooden name necklace for each child. A great way to begin your first day of class—with a present!

Getting To Know Parents

Save scraps of paper, yarn, cloth, stickers, wrapping paper, and other decorative materials. Place the bits and pieces in a lunch bag along with some pictures of Jewish symbols and ritual objects. Prepare one bag for each child *and his or her parents.*

When parents arrive with their children, give each family a paper bag of materials. Have available glue, crayons, and large sheets of colored construction paper. Ask each family to make a collage titled "Our Jewish Family." While the families are working, move around the room, meeting and talking with the parents. You will end up with colorful artwork to display, and you also will have met your students' parents in an informal, relaxed atmosphere.

Bean Bag or Ball Toss

You will need either a bean bag or a medium-size beach ball, as well as a name tag for each student. Form a circle of the students. Using the bean bag or ball, call out a student's name and toss the bean bag or ball to that student. After the first toss, explain to the children they are to call the name of a student and toss the bean bag or ball to that child. Continue with the toss until everyone has had a chance to toss the bean bag or ball.

Balloons

Prepare different "getting-to-know-you" questions, one per student, on small pieces of colorful paper. Roll up each slip tightly and slip it into a balloon. Blow up the balloons and attach one to each student's chair with colorful yarn—it makes for a festive welcome! Think of the fun the children will have when you tell them each to burst the balloon, read the question, and share the response with the whole class.

A Warm Welcome to Young Students

Prepare a lunch bag for each student with some of the following items: cotton ball, rubber band, paper clip, a gold foil Jewish star, gold piece of yarn, penny, a piece of chocolate, candy corn, or anything that you can tie together. Include a note that explains the meaning of each item, such as:

Paper clip: to remind you that we all are together and care for each other
Jewish star: to remind you that you are a special Jewish person
Cotton ball: to remind you that we give out "warm fuzzies" (kind words and warm feelings)
Yarn: to remind you that we are all one
Penny: to remind you that you are valuable and special
Chocolate: for when you need a hug
Candy corn: to remind you that we need a sense of humor

These are just a few items that can be put in the bag, but there are certainly others.

Roll of Toilet Paper or M&Ms

Pass a roll of toilet paper or M&Ms around the class and tell the children to each take one to five pieces. Then, one at a time, each child is to tell one piece of information about himself or herself for each M&M or tissue square taken. If you are using M&Ms, you can have them take one of each color and ask specific questions for each color.

Example: Yellow: What is your name?
Blue: Where do you live?
Brown: Who are the people in your family?

Then go around the room and have each child eat the color that corresponds to each question.

Acrostic ID Cards

Invite students to print their name down the left side of an index card vertically in capital letters. Each letter of their name is then used as the beginning of a statement or phrase that tells the class something about that student. For example:

Yellow is my favorite color.
Once I went to Legoland.
Never eats peas.
I'm seven years old.

The child then can draw a small self-portrait and sign the ID card, after which each student introduces himself or herself using his or her new ID card.

A Hand Tells a Lot

Give each student a blank, letter-size sheet of paper and colored markers. Ask students to draw an outline of their hand on the paper. Next, have them fill in each one of the fingers with five words that they think describes who they are. Then, around the hand outline, ask each student to draw pictures of objects that represent either the artist or things the child does well. Ask each child to sign his or her "hand" and to share the work with the class.

Surveys

Do some brainstorming with the class to create a list of questions students could use to get to know one another better. Together, choose five questions from the list. Ask students to choose a partner, or pair them up so they are with some one they do not know well. Have each student survey the other and then introduce their "new friend" to the rest of the class.

Name a Jewish Holiday

Have the children sit in a circle. Tell the students they are to introduce themselves with their name and the name of their favorite Jewish holiday, for example, "My name is David and my favorite Jewish holiday is Chanukah." The next student does the same, naming his or her favorite Jewish holiday, but also repeats the information that came before ("This is David and his favorite holiday is Chanukah"). Continue going around the circle with each child repeating the names that came before.

Puzzles

When students arrive, give each a 12 x 18 piece of card stock or construction paper as well as an envelope containing instructions to create a poster that tells all about the child. Invite them to place a title at the top of the sheet— for example, "All about Leah." Have each student create a colorful poster that tells about his or her favorite activities, hobbies, Jewish songs, holidays, family, pets, siblings, and so forth. The completed poster is then cut into puzzle pieces and placed in the envelope. The title of the poster should be written on the envelope. Students then exchange envelopes with a classmate, and the pairs assemble their puzzles together. The pairs then use the information from these puzzle posters to introduce each other to the whole class.

A Rather Unique Puzzle

Once you know how many students you will have, create a blank poster-size jigsaw puzzle. Choose a theme, for example, favorite Jewish holiday, favorite Hebrew letter, or favorite activity. When your students arrive, give each student a piece of the puzzle to decorate.

Have an empty bulletin board and thumbtacks available. When they have completed decorating the puzzle pieces, have students assemble the puzzle on the bulletin board, using the thumbtacks to attach the pieces. As they do so, each student should describe what his or her puzzle piece represents. Once the puzzle has been put together, you can explain that it represents unity. When a student misbehaves or disturbs the class, remove his or her puzzle piece. This will illustrate that behavior affects not only the student, it also affects the entire class. The class is not whole unless the class is together. As in Judaism, if we do not work together, we are not whole.

Colorful Tables

This activity is good for young children. Cover the tables with white butcher paper, and place crayons or markers on top. As children arrive, tell them to choose a table and begin to draw their first impressions of school, what they like to do, their feelings about being there, and so forth. This will keep students busy while the parents leave.

"Fortune Cookie" Hunt

Using fortune cookie–size strips of paper, have the students write down such clues as what they do well, favorite Jewish activity, favorite sport or game, or names of family members—about all that will fit on such a small piece of paper. Have each student place his or her slip of paper in a small film canister (usually free at photo shops). Mix them all up in a box. One by one, students pick out a canister and read the clues, then the whole class tries to guess which student is being described.

Breakfast Sale

Before school begins, send a letter home asking students to bring in big, clean cereal boxes that are not torn. You'll also need drawing paper the size of the box (since cereal boxes are different sizes, you may need to trim the paper), scissors, markers, and glue.

After the children have arrived, talk about how attractive the cereal boxes look. Tell students they are to create their own cereal boxes to sell themselves! Each student should include on the box his or her name and nickname; a logo; the names of family members (including pets); a favorite sport or game; something he or she does well; a favorite Jewish activity, holiday, and song; and anything else he or she wants others to know. Students should be sure to include at least one picture or photograph. Students share their completed boxes with one another and use the boxes to introduce one another to the class.

Storefront Sale

Discuss how stores display their goods in their windows, emphasizing their best items. Give the students drawing paper and markers and ask them to design a "store window" in which they will be selling themselves. Students should show what is important about them, adding pictures and colors to display themselves at their very best!

Wave Your Flag!

You will need construction paper, popsicle sticks, tape, and crayons or markers. Give each student a sheet of construction paper, a popsicle stick, some tape, and markers or crayons. (You may want to have students first outline their flag on scratch paper.) Have each student design a flag that tells all the good things about himself or herself. Give students time to stand up and wave their flags to introduce themselves to the rest of the class.

Musical Name Cards

Prepare a number of cards, one for each student in the class, with varying directions, for example:

- Find out Steven's favorite Jewish holiday.
- Find out Michelle's favorite color.
- Find out Joseph's favorite Jewish song.

Place the cards in a small bag. Have the children wear name tags and sit in a circle. Play some music while students pass the bag around the circle. When you stop the music, the child holding the bag picks out a card and follows the directions. Continue playing until every child has had a turn.

Auto-Body-Biographies

For each child you will need a brown paper bag, several colorful strips of 3 x 11 paper, markers, and three sheets of white paper. You will also need a Poloraid camera and enough film to take one picture of each child.

Take head shots of the children as they arrive. Give each child some markers and the strips of paper. Ask children to write on each strip an important Jewish event in their life, using only one side of the paper. These events could be anything from family Shabbat experiences, bar or bat mitzvah ceremonies, Pesach seders, Chanukah and Purim celebrations, and so on. Place each child's finished strips in his or her paper bag. Group students into pairs. Partners take turns picking the strips of paper and telling each other about the special Jewish times in their life.

After going through the papers, students write a short autobiography, using the other side of the paper strips. When completed, give each child his or her photograph and two sheets of white paper. Have students glue the picture to one sheet and draw feet on the second sheet. They attach their written autobiography between the two sheets. Hang these "auto-body-biographies" around the room for everyone to read.

Names on a Stick

Do your students have trouble remembering classmates' names? Try this: On one end of an individual craft stick write the name of each child in the class. Decorate a coffee can (with a Jewish theme, of course!) and place the sticks in the can "name down." Form a circle of the class. Ask one student to pick a stick out of the can and read the name, then give the stick to you (the teacher) and take the can to the child whose name was just read. Play continues until there are no more sticks left in the box.

Class Survey

On a sheet of paper, draw a grid of sixteen squares. In each square, write a phrase that describes one or more of your students. Some suggestions are:

Likes the Sabbath
Knows what a *Havdalah* candle is
Is good at reading Hebrew

Is already a bar or bat mitzvah

Knows when Pesach is

Has a birthday on a Jewish holiday

Knows whom he or she is named for

Has recently read a book about Israel

Has a great idea for a new Jewish holiday

Has his or her own *Kiddush* cup

Can sing a Hebrew song

Is able to recite *Birkat HaMazon*

Students then circulate around the room and find those who match the statements, writing the person's name in the appropriate box. There should be only one name to each statement, even though there may be more than one match. When students have finished, bring everyone together in a circle. Introduce one another and see how many matches were made with each person.

Finding the Talent in Your Classroom

Let the kids develop a class résumé of their talents. Prepare a list of what would be required for such a class résumé. Include hobbies, talents, and bodies of knowledge. For example:

____ plays a musical instrument.

____ has good writing skills.

____ is knowledgeable about _____.

____ is a good actor.

Divide the class into small groups. Tell the students they have a vast amount of talent, and the best way to discover what talent is available is to develop a class résumé. Remind them that they want to identify *all* the talent and acknowledge the class's resources. Give the groups time to complete their résumés. Bring the groups together and compile a composite list of all the skills found within the class. You might even want to celebrate all the talent found within the entire group.

Classroom Management

Even if you only meet once or twice a week, you need to have some semblance of order in the classroom, with rules that have been developed by you and the students. It is important that these rules be established at the very beginning of the year.

The talmudic Sage Hillel once said, "what is hateful to yourself do not unto others" (Babylonian Talmud *Shabbat* 31a). Similar to this is: "If you don't have something nice to say about someone, don't say anything." Our students often purposefully use words that hurt. Whatever the reason, it is our job to provide a positive Jewish model.

L'SHON HARA

L'shon hara is the Jewish term for speech that includes putting people down, telling tales about people, and gossiping. As you develop your rules for the class-room, be sure to include "no *l'shon hara*" on the list, even if the students them-selves do not suggest it. You might use one or two of the following activities to help students understand why it is so important for "no *l'shon hara*" to be includ-ed. (Other activities can be found in the "Jewish Values, Concepts, and Symbols" sections of this book.) Introduce your students to the rabbinic ideas that *l'shon hara* was as bad as murder (Jerusalem Talmud, *Pei-ah* 1:1). Ask them to discuss this teaching and to explain why they agreed or disagree.

Picture Book

Either obtain a picture of each child from the family or take a picture of each child the first day of school. Explain to the students that it will be used to create a special book. Place each picture at the top of a blank sheet of paper, then place all the sheets in a loose-leaf notebook. Tell students that they will take turns writ-ing something nice about all the other students. Pass out each sheet to the stu-dents and have them write about the person on the sheet before them. Next have them pass the sheet to the next person so that everyone writes about someone new. Remind them that they are to write only something nice about that person. Continue until every person has written something nice about another student. Leave the book out for the students to read during free time and to add to it if they desire. From time to time during the year, when students sometimes forget about the no *l'shon hara* rule, take the book out and let them look at it again to remind them how special it is to read something nice about one another.

Another One

Ask the students to search through the news and see how many articles they can find with examples of people saying nice things about others, for example, prais-ing others for their efforts or admiring an artist's work. Have each student bring in one or two articles to share. After the class has done so, create a bulletin board with the heading "Kindness Makes the News."

One More

Prepare a sheet of paper. Down the left hand side, list the names of all the students in the class with several spaces between each name. Pass the sheets to each student. Then tell them to write the nicest thing they can say about each person next to his or her name. When finished, gather up the papers. At home, write each student's name on a separate sheet of paper. On each sheet, copy what others have said about that person. Make a copy for each student. At the next class session, hand each student the appropriate paper. Watch the reactions when students read what nice things have been said about them!

Be a Kindness Star

This is a nice way to end a class. Sitting in a circle, go around the circle and ask each student to say something nice to the person on the right. It could be about something the student did to help out, or maybe a compliment about a hairstyle or shirt. Tell the students they are all kindness stars for being so kind to one another.

ROLE MODELING

Modeling Jewish Values

Years ago when I was still teaching in the classroom, working with the youth group, and doing weekend camp programs, I realized one of the best ways to teach young people Jewish values was to practice the values. By simply living your Jewish values, you are providing the kids with a good example. Some little activities go a long way, too. Here are just a few suggestions for modeling a Jewish lifestyle:

Participate in your synagogue's Mitzvah Day.
Write a letter to the editor.
Attend Shabbat services on a regular basis.
Gather food for a food pantry or prepare a meal for a soup kitchen.
Tell stories about the special things your family does on Jewish holidays.
Display bumper stickers having a message about a Jewish value.

Demonstrate for a cause you believe in.
Bring in *tzedakah* for the class *tzedakah* box.

Practice What You Preach! Don't be hypocritical or inconsistent. The students will see when you say one thing and do another. For example, suppose the students read that we are to leave the corners of the field for the poor. You encourage the students to develop a food-drive program for the synagogue. The students work hard, gathering, sorting, and packing cans of food—but you bring nothing and do nothing. What lesson are you teaching the children? If you spend time teaching prayer or about Shabbat, do the kids ever see you at Shabbat services? After encouraging students to respect others, do you choose your favorites in the class or treat the students like babies?

To be a good role model you need to be sincere and really listen—not act authoritarian. Communicate your commitment through actions. Be honest with yourself: is your behavior consistent with the Jewish values you teach? Take students' feedback seriously. Are your deeds matching your words? Admit you are wrong—don't pretend to be perfect. If you lose your temper or act improperly, acknowledge your error.

Role Models from the Bible

The Bible offers us a number of good role models:

Abraham and Sarah welcome strangers into their tent.
Ruth demonstrates loyalty and devotion to Naomi.
Joseph forgives his brothers for what they did to him.

There are also some negative role models—a good way to teach what not to be like:

Jacob chooses favorites among his children.
David wants to marry Batsheva and has her husband killed.
Cain kills his brother, Abel.

Those are just a few examples of role modeling you will find in the Bible. Why not let the students find some more? Invite volunteers to explain their choices (being sure to identify the type of role model the figure makes).

In the Classroom

FORMING GROUPS

Here are a number of ways to form groups.

Cards

Once you have decided on the number of groups you will need, take index cards and place a colored adhesive dot on each card. Use a different color for each group. You also can use themed decorative stickers—for example, animals, flowers, or Jewish symbols. Give a coded card to each student as you hand out materials. This enables you to place the students in groupings of your choice. Assign each group a work station. You may wish to label the various work areas with an additional coded card.

Or for older students, try the following variations.

Match Up

Create a list of names of people who go together, for example: Moses, Miriam, and Aaron; or David, Saul, and Solomon. Place their names on index cards and pass them out to the students. Students then match them up with the other members of the class. You could also use holidays, Israeli cities, and so forth.

Draw Numbers

Place numbers on individual slips of paper for the number of groups you need and have students draw a slip of paper. Each student becomes a member of that numbered group.

TAKING ATTENDANCE

Take a picture of each student. Cut and glue each picture to a sturdy metal disk—the metal ends of frozen juice cans work well for this. On the back of each disk place a strip of magnetic tape. Each class period, place on the chalkboard a statement that can be answered by a simple "yes" or "no," and create columns accordingly. When students arrive they look at the statement and, based on his or her answer, places the name tag in the appropriate column. At a glance, you can see who is present and who is absent. You can send the magnets home at the end of the school year.

Clothespin Names

Write each child's name on a clothespin. Divide a strip of oak tag in two, labeling one side "Here" (or *Po*) and the other "Absent" (or *Lo Po*). Clip the clothespins to the "Absent" side. As a student arrives, the child moves his or her clothespin to the "Here" side.

Roll Call Questions

Place a question with many possible answers on the board. As the students arrive, explain that they are to think of a creative answer, or they should do some quick research in the classroom to find the answer. The question can be based on your unit of study or on current events, and require either a factual answer or the student's opinion.

As you call role, ask each student to respond with his or her answers. It can be fun for everyone and keeps the students busy as others are arriving.

SOME RECYCLING TIPS

Mittens

Fill an old or orphaned mitten with dried beans and sew the wrist closed with heavy yarn. You'll have a beanbag to use for a variety of creative games.

Rainy Day Boxes

Collect scraps of materials, magazines, buttons, glitter, straws, raw dry pasta, and glue. Store them in boxes, identifying what is in each box. Encourage students to make their own contributions. All these items can be used for a variety of art projects.

Old Umbrellas

Need some wall space? Get someone to hang a hook from your ceiling. Take the material off an old umbrella and hang it, inverted, from the hook. Now you can use each spoke to hang mobiles, art work, and whatever else you want to display. Just be sure your ceilings are high enough!

Ice Cube Trays

The inexpensive plastic ones make great paint containers. They will hold small amounts of many different colors.

Vinyl Placemats

These make durable game boards. You can draw a game trail right on the placemat using a permanent marker, or glue on a paper game design and cover with clear contact paper. They are easy to clean and store.

Plastic Liquid Detergent Bottles

These make great storage bottles for paint. Prepare different colors of powdered tempera paints. Pour each individual color in one of these bottles and label. When you need a small amount, just shake and pour!

Cardboard Milk Cartons

Cut the top off two cartons and push the bottoms together. Cover with contact paper and you have a nice sturdy building block.

Storage Containers

Empty baby wipes containers make great storage boxes, and they have a snap lid so that nothing can spill out. Metal bandage boxes all have snap lids and can be used to store crayons.

Game Pieces

Buttons make good game pieces. Candy works even better. Try using wrapped candy as markers—students can eat the pieces after the game is finished. (Use sugarless candy if you are concerned about the sugar.) For bingo, try using jelly beans, candy corn, or raisins.

Game Spinners

Take a margarine tub with a lid. You will also need a brass fastener and a large safety pin. Using a waterproof marker, divide the lid into sections and number them. Place the fastener through the loop in the safety pin. Make a small hole in the top of the plastic lid. Insert the fastener through the hole and secure it. You now have a spinner and a tub to hold the game pieces.

Stencils

I don't know about you, but when I save margarine tubs and plastic sour cream containers, for some reason I always end up with extra lids. These lids can be transformed into sturdy stencils for any fun art activity. For example, use them to make placemats, holiday cards, challah covers, collages (cut designs from old magazines).

Just take the lid and draw a simple outline of the desired shape on the underside. With a utility knife, cut out the shape. You can cut off the rim of the lid if you wish. To use the stencil, tape the lid to a sheet of paper or card stock. Dip a piece of sponge into poster paint and dab lightly inside the cutout space. Let dry, then lift the stencil carefully to avoid any smearing. Because the stencil is plastic it can be washed and used again.

A Tip for the Future

Some arts and crafts activities require simple materials found around the house. At the beginning of the year, prepare a list of those supplies you will be needing, or anticipate needing, and send a letter home to the parents asking them to help out with some of these craft supplies. Your list might include such items as egg cartons, baby food jars or other jars with lids, sponges, craft sticks, cardboard tubes, paper plates, laundry detergent or powdered drink scoops, aluminum pie pans, hangers, empty film canisters, and yogurt or powdered drink containers.

TEACHING TIPS

Write a Story

Make your lesson come alive! Based on your unit of study, write a short story using your students' names for those of the characters in the story. Be sure to include everyone. Make copies for each student. Imagine their faces as they find themselves in the story!

Torah Study Tip

When studying a Torah portion, choose one concept to emphasize. Each *parashah* usually has so many different concepts and ideas that to study them all would be confusing to the student. Consider, for example, *Parashat Shoftim* (Deuteronomy 16:18–21:9). This *parashah* covers a variety of laws regarding the Jewish legal system, the monarchy, prophecy, cities of refuge, murder, boundaries, sacrifices, legal witnesses, and war. One concept is the admonition in time of war not to cut down the enemy's trees, especially those that produce food (Deuteronomy 20:19–20). Even younger children can understand this concept. After reading the text (or a simplified version thereof) ask students: What would the reasons be for not cutting down any trees? What happens when there are no trees? How long does it take new trees to grow? How difficult would it be to replace them? As a project, have the students make a list of all the different trees from which we get food. They could also make a mural showing all these different trees and pictures of the food that comes from each tree.

Background Music

Feel free to play background music that is related to the topic of your lesson plan.

Journal Writing

There are a lot of reasons for students to keep journals. Keeping a journal is a way of recording personal feelings we may or may not want to communicate to others. When introducing students to the use of journals, remind them it is almost like a diary. Give them a few minutes at the end of each class to write in their journals. Encourage students to record their observations and reactions, something special that might have happened that day or what they want to remember about the lesson.

Alternative

After a reading assignment, tell the students to take the role of one of the characters in the material. Have students write one or two journal entries as though they were that person, letting their imagination run loose. Invite students to share their journal entries when they have finished to give them a wider perspective.

Create a Jewish Museum

This is a project that can be done by one class, several classes, or the entire school. It invites the students to participate behind the scenes in the creation of a model Jewish museum. Your Jewish museum project will involve arts, crafts, research, writing, and, most of all, imagination. As you begin to plan, keep in mind that there are all kinds of museums—some are collections of art, some of artifacts, and some of glass, just to name a few. The Museum of the Jewish Diaspora in Tel Aviv is a history of the travels of the Jewish people. There are also many Holocaust museums, and in Jerusalem, the Israel Museum is dedicated to artifacts from Israel's past and present. So, you have many options. Where to begin?

Once you have determined who is going to be involved with the project, the students will first need to know what a museum is and what it contains. This introduction to learning about museums will depend on the age and knowledge of your students. Adjust the following accordingly:

1. See if anyone has visited a museum. Ask these students to tell about their visit. Where was the museum? What kind of museum—nature, art, and so on—was it? How were objects displayed? What was the highlight of the visit? What impressed them the most?

2. Talk about collections—that *is* what a museum is—and about what people collect. See if any of the students collect anything: stones, stamps, baseball cards, bottlecaps, and so forth.

3. The next step is to talk about what the children will be collecting for their Jewish museum. Keep in mind, though, that what they collect will coincide with your unit of study.

4. Identify a location for your museum. If it is just your class, the choice is simple—your classroom becomes the museum site. If more than one class will be involved, you could designate each classroom as a specific area of the museum. If the whole school is involved, you could designate a specific area in each classroom, creating a walking tour from one classroom to the next. Or use your synagogue's entry or social hall. The museum could go around the wall of the entire room.

5. Get the parents involved in the project. This is big enough for everyone to take part. Identify people who can sew, help with artwork, or set up displays. A docent from a local museum would be great! Draw on the resources you have right in your own congregation, then have fun!

6. Gather objects. Since what you gather will depend on your unit of study, the following are some examples of the kinds of things your class could

be collecting for the museum. Some items will have to be made in arts and crafts sessions, some designed and written up based on students' findings, and some will have to be imagined. Encourage the students to be creative. Your museum might include the following:

- *Items that belonged to someone in Jewish history:* Joseph's many-colored coat, Moses' staff, the *mishkan,* ritual objects, photographs, postage stamps, postcards, any other artifacts from the past.
- *Items that tell something about the time and place in which people lived:* old coins, oil lamps, clothes, artwork, tapestries, books, pottery, and so on.
- *Things that may or may not be very old but that provide insight into history:* replicas of synagogues or shtetls; dishes, pottery, and glassware; maps, furniture, ship models; illustrations of means of travel, and so on.
- *Things that are new:* student-designed and -created ritual objects like *chanukiyot,* candlesticks, challah covers, seder plates, *Kiddush* cups, and so on.

As you can see from these sample lists, you have many options. I think the most important element will be your unit of study. Suppose your Jewish museum will be developed by several classes. One class may be studying Israel, another immigration of Jews to America, and another American Jewish history. Think of all the options that are open to your students, for example:

- *Israel:* Postage stamps, postcards, a replica of the *Kotel,* layout replica of a kibbutz, replicas of mosaic floors, a seven-branch menorah, any religious items, pictures of flora and fauna, pottery shards.
- *Things related to American Jewish history:* Here there are even more options. What about focusing on your own Jewish community? Get pictures, artwork, Jewish artifacts. Most important, though, are the interviews of Jewish people who have made contributions to the growth of the community.
- *Synagogue history:* Or, you could just take the synagogue and center your museum around it. Who founded it? Who was the first rabbi? Prepare a display of the different rabbis who have served the synagogue. Include pictures of events taking place at the synagogue, or old pictures of different events. Get members of the congregation to help with this. Create archives that include copies of letters and official

papers. Don't forget the newspapers—they could be a source of information about the community and synagogue.

- *Symbols of immigration:* Students interview their parents, grandparents, relatives, and older members of the congregation. Collect pictures of people getting off the boat at Ellis Island, or follow the travels of a new immigrant when he or she comes to the United States. Where did immigrants begin their travels, and where did they finally settle? Students might need to use their creative imagination, but as long is it is a result of their research, that is fine. They can make it as realistic as they want, creating postcards from foreign countries or letters to and from family members who might have remained behind.

I have given you just a few ideas of what can be collected. I am sure you will, with your students, come up with some more, especially when you become involved in your studies. When the students know about the project, they will automatically be looking for items and ideas to include in their portion of the museum.

Brown-bag It

Children are naturally curious. This technique will help stimulate some thought while creating excitement to begin the lesson. On each student's desk, place a brown paper sack that has been stapled shut. These mysterious bags (which need to be prepared in advance) can contain items related to the upcoming lesson plan. For example, for a lesson on Shabbat, you might place in each bag a plastic wine goblet, a candle, and a small roll. As children arrive, invite them to manipulate the bag to try and figure out what is in it. Give students a chance to open the bag. As you go through your lesson, students can take out the appropriate item. This will keep them thinking about the topic, and they will look forward to "using" the items found in the bag. Allow children to decorate their bags and to take them home to share with family members.

Treasure or Scavenger Hunts—Some Tips

These activities are not only fun, but can be a good way to introduce new material. Because treasure hunts take time both to prepare and to do, they are best used to introduce a new unit, rather than simply a new lesson.

Treasure and scavenger hunts can be used anywhere in your curriculum. For example, have a treasure hunt to introduce a unit on the Torah. Students can learn how to look through the Torah and how to use it. Have them search for certain names, places, verses, or Hebrew words. Or, use a treasure hunt to introduce your study of Israel. Using a detailed map, students can find where cities, mountains, and important sites are located.

Some Tips for Planning a Treasure Hunt

1. Make your clues challenging, but not impossible. Keep in mind the age of your students and make sure the clues are age-appropriate.
2. If your students like crossword puzzles, write clues that require filling in the blanks.
3. Create rebuses by using words and pictures cut from old magazines.
4. Write your clues on white paper with a white crayon! Then give the student washable colored markers. Drawing on the paper with the markers will make the words visible.
5. Use a number code by assigning a number (1–26) to each letter of the alphabet. Then write your clues using numbers.
6. Write short rhyming riddles that the students have to solve to find the treasure.

Storytelling and Art

A few summers ago my granddaughters went to a summer art camp. When we were visiting them, the oldest one showed us her art work. The first picture was rather strange, and I asked her what it represented. She told me that it was a picture of how Yochanan ben Zakkai escaped from Jerusalem. She pointed out the rabbi lying in the coffin, the two younger rabbis carrying it, and Jerusalem in the background. She proceeded to tell me the whole story of how ben Zakkai escaped and how he set up the school at Yavneh. I was amazed!

The next picture was a scene of people sitting at a dinner table and I asked her what the story was behind this picture. Again, she proceeded to tell me about a rabbi and his driver and how they traded places. I knew the story and listened intently and was again amazed because she even got the punch line correct!

The lesson here is: tell the story and then let the children draw their interpretation of the story. (By the way, my granddaughter was seven years old when this took place.)

STORYTELLING IN THE CLASSROOM

Sharing our lives through storytelling helps us learn about other people.

Some Suggestions

Here are a few ideas for ways to involve students in storytelling:

Share life stories of family members based on interviews.
Create travel advertisements.
Write letters to or from story characters.
Rewrite a story in a different form.
Dress up as a character in a story and role-play that part.
Use puppets to act out a story.
Make a story quilt.
Write stories and make class books of these stories.
Design posters, book covers, and ads for a story.
Invite parents, grandparents, or congregation members to class to tell stories.

HELPFUL ACTIVITIES TO ENRICH READING ASSIGNMENTS

Teachers often give students material to read. However, reading assignments don't work unless you give the students a task to perform that stems from the reading. What follows are some new ideas to make reading more productive:

A Story Tree

Use this activity for any reading assignment that you give to the entire class. Draw an outline of a tree on a sheet of paper. Place numbered lines 1–8 from the top to the bottom in the center of the tree, leaving enough room for the students to write their answers. To the side of the tree outline, list statements that the students are to respond to by filling in the blank spaces. Then divide your class into small groups so students can work together to complete this task.

Your statements could include the following:

1. Write the name of the story's main character.
2. List two words that describe the main character.
3. List three words that describe the setting or location.

4. List four words that explain the problem encountered.
5. List five words that describe one event in the story.
6. List six words that describe another event.
7. List seven words that describe the main event.
8. List eight words that state the solution to the problem.

Upon completion of the story tree, each group shares its responses, comparing differences and similarities.

Mobiles

Have students draw, color, and cut out shapes of characters, symbols, or ritual objects related to their assignment. Punch a hole in the top of each character and tie with a string or piece of yarn. Hang the cutouts on a hanger from the ceiling.

Big Books

Let each student choose a character or object from the reading. Have the student draw a big picture of it on oak tag, color it, and then cut it out. Use it as a cover for several more pages cut out of paper the same shape. Have the student write what he or she learned from this character or object, what he or she would like to teach this character, and any other observations the student would like to include. Allow time for students to share their books with one another.

Act It Out

Divide the class into small groups. Give each group a different but related reading assignment. For example, the readings could all be on the same subject, with each presenting a different perspective or describing a different person or event. Challenge the students in each group to speak as a person in the event, perhaps even dressing up in clothes of that time period.

Great Mural

This is especially good for lower-grade students. Take a huge piece of butcher paper (white is best) and place it on the wall or the floor (whichever is better for the students to work). Let the students create a giant wall mural that depicts an event they have just read about. You might wish to assign each student a specific moment in the event. If students work in "chronological order," you will then have an artistic historical record. Hang it outside the classroom for others to see.

Reports

Once students have read the assigned material, divide the class into pairs or small groups. Each group is to design a complete advertising campaign for both print and broadcast media about the material the members have just read. Students can prepare press releases as well. Have students present their campaigns to the class.

Round Robin

Divide the class into small groups. Give the groups the reading assignment, then give out these different tasks, one to each group:

1. Design a large poster that contains the major elements of what students have read so others can learn what they have discovered. Provide the class with the necessary materials.
2. Write a short story that relates the major elements of what students have read.
3. Create a short play that dramatizes the major elements of what they have read.

Each group makes its presentation to the others.

Talk Show Hosts

Divide the class into pairs. Give each pair a different reading assignment on the same subject matter. The two are to read the material individually, then create questions they would ask the author if they could interview him or her. Then have one student act as the interviewer and the other as the author. Invite them to role-play before the class, with the interviewer asking the questions of the author, who answers so the class can learn more about what the pair has read.

A Reading Scavenger Hunt

Divide the class into small groups. Give each group a different reading assignment. Prior to the activity, prepare a list of "items" each group must find during their reading. However, don't just list people or events. Rather, create clues that students can use to identify the most important points of their reading selection. For instance, readings might be about different ideas about God or different ways to celebrate a holiday. When they have completed their scavenger hunt, ask students to share their results with the rest of the class. This way the other students will learn about the material, as well.

Post Cards

Give each student a postcard-size piece of card stock or blank index card. Have the student draw a picture that represents a highlight of the reading. On the back of the card the student is to write a message about the picture on the front of the card. Invite students to share their cards with the class.

Book Cover

Fold a piece of paper over to look like a book jacket. Students then draw a picture on the front that represents the highlight of their reading. On the inside front section, students write a short descriptive paragraph of the highlights. On the back cover, students draw a picture of the main character, person, or event from the reading, then write a short descriptive paragraph on the inside back section. Display the book jackets on the table.

Alternative: Paper Bag Show-and-Tell

After members have finished reading their assignment, give each group a paper bag. Tell them to place three to five objects in the bag that relate to what they have read. They can be real objects, photographs, or pictures from magazines or catalogs. Members can decorate the outside of the bag, if they desire. Each group then gives a presentation about its reading assignment, using the objects in the bag.

Alternative: Pictures from Many Colors

Give each student a large piece of white drawing paper. Tell the children to paint or color it with no design—just to cover the entire sheet with colors as a background. Let it dry. Then, provide students with pencils and blank paper, scissors, glue, and construction paper. On the blank paper, students draw outlines of what they want to cut from the construction paper to make a picture. Once they have decided what images they wish to place on their brightly colored background, children can trace them on the construction paper. When they have drawn all their images, students cut them out and glue them to their background. Invite students to share the results with the class.

TRY THESE QUICKIES

Here are a few more useful suggestions.

Attention, Please!

Want students' attention? Use a kazoo!

Record Teachable Moments

Keep handy one of those inexpensive disposable cameras to capture such moments.

A Big Glass Jar

Place a Jewish artifact inside and tell the students to write a short story about it.

A Big Book of Jewish Holidays

Your class can create a book of Jewish holidays. Include prayers, recipes, games, art work, and so on. Give it to the young children in the lower grades or to the school or synagogue library.

Holiday Wall

Outside of your classroom, cover a good portion of the wall with butcher paper. Hang several watercolor markers along the wall. Encourage children and adults to decorate the paper with holiday messages.

EVALUATING LESSON PLANS

Ask the Students

Before school is out, take some time to talk to your students. Let them do an evaluation of the class. Get feedback about what worked and what changes need to be made. Students are your best critics. As long as they know you are really interested in improving the classroom experience, most students will be honest.

Ask Other Teachers

Meet with other teachers and go over the lessons that need improvement. Brainstorm ideas to make the lessons more viable. Keep in mind that two heads are better than one, and meeting with other teachers gives you an opportunity to help one another.

Long-Range Planning

Organize Those Lesson Plans

Now is the best time to gather up all those lessons—even the little scraps of paper on which you wrote notes about what to do for the day when you didn't have time to create a proper lesson plan.

1. Take the scraps of paper and write out the lesson plan as you should have done. Since you have already conducted the lesson, you now have the opportunity to make any changes that will make it even better. Of course, if the lesson was not successful, think about what went wrong with it. How did the kids react? What seemed to be missing? Does the lesson just need some minor changes, or do you have to rethink the whole plan? If necessary write a new lesson plan while you have the time. Review your other, prepared lessons the same way. When reading over the lesson plans, ask yourself: How does this lesson connect the student to the outside world? That is always one of the most important elements of a lesson and often overlooked.

2. Place *all* the lesson plans in their proper order. If you have not yet placed them in a notebook or file, now is the time to do so. Be sure to include any accompanying handouts, parent letters, and so forth. Prepare files of ideas and activities on different subject areas. Be specific! Keep separate files for individual holidays or prayers, for different periods of Jewish history or cities and sites in Israel, for each weekly Torah portion. This will help you plan your lessons more efficiently.

3. As you receive additional teaching ideas or materials, file them in the appropriate place. If necessary, cut them out and tape them to a larger sheet of paper so they don't get lost. Or, glue related short ideas on one sheet of paper. Before you know it you will have a wealth of ideas as resources.

4. Make a list of all the supplies you will be needing for your lessons. See that your principal gets this list well in advance of the beginning of school for next year.

Learn from One Another

It would be wonderful if, at least once a month during the summer, all the teachers in your school got together to share their success and their failures. Educators could use this time to brainstorm for new ideas; and it's also a good time for old teachers to meet new teachers. Choose a time that is convenient for most of your teachers. Begin the session with a *d'var Torah,* asking a different teacher to do this each time. Ask each teacher to bring at least one successful lesson he or she did this past year to share with the other teachers. During the meeting, ask each teacher to explain why the lesson worked. Make copies of the lessons for all the teachers. Just imagine all the different ideas that will be shared!

For each session, you might choose a theme, perhaps a subject that one or more teachers are having problems with, to brainstorm. A group of teachers can come up with more ideas than just one person can.

Need Help in the Classroom?

Now is a good time to create and work on a *madrichim* program. Identify those teens interested in working in the religious school. Conduct training during the summer so that they can become more than just extra hands and eyes. Here are some things to do:

1. Teach your *madrichim* tutoring skills so they can work with students who need assistance with Hebrew or who are below grade level in reading and need extra help with a project.
2. Train *madrichim* to work with the advanced students on special projects. You never have enough time to work with gifted students who need to be challenged.
3. Demonstrate how to work with learning centers, stations based on a theme, two kids studying a text, or a group of kids writing a play.
4. Explain how to work with special needs students who are mainstreamed into the classroom.

The Madrikhim Handbook: A Training Program for Teenagers Working in Jewish Schools, by Rabbi Samuel Joseph (Los Angeles: Torah Aura, 1990), is an invaluable resource.

LONG-TERM PROJECTS AND PLANS

Many projects can run the entire year, or for several weeks during the year. Now is the time to go over your calendar and determine when these projects will begin and end. Consider some of the following.

Tzedakah

Plan a "penny harvest" in which children of all ages collect pennies during the entire year. At the end of the year they determine where the money is to go. Write to Ziv Tzedakah Fund, 384 Wyoming Ave, Millburn, NJ 07041, to obtain a listing of some very different funds that can use monetary assistance. This list goes beyond the usual organizations with which we are most familiar.

Deeds of Loving-Kindness

Encourage the students to be kind to others. Create a Kindness Tree—it can either be a big branch or a large piece of butcher paper with the outline of a tree, but with no leaves. Cut out "leaves" in bright colors. Each time a child does a kind deed or mitzvah, he or she gets to place a Kindness leaf on the tree. By the end of the school year the tree will be full of leaves!

Plays, Music, Art, Museums

Review your calendar to see what special events could take place during the year. A play for Purim? Identify the play now. Special music for Pesach? Determine what is available and what you will use now. What art projects do you want to do? Make your plans now! Want to create a museum as part of a unit of study? Identify the different sections of the museum and decide how objects will be displayed now. Or, do you want to plan a visit to a local museum? Make the arrangements now.

Any plans you make now will make your school year that much easier and less harried.

Getting to Know Your Students Better

It would be helpful to come into your classroom with some knowledge about your students before the school year begins. It is not too difficult to do. Obtain a class list from the school office as soon as it is available. Address the envelopes to each family by hand. (People often ignore letters having preprinted labels.) Then, with the permission of the educator, prepare a survey to send to the parents. Your survey can include such things like:

What have been some of the best experiences your child has had in religious school?

What have been some of the negative experiences your child has had?

What special events will your family be celebrating this year?

What are some of your child's strengths?

What are some of your child's weaknesses?

What special interests does your child have?

What do you think is your child's learning style?

Does your child work best alone or with others?

Assure parents that the information they give you is confidential. Include a self-addressed stamped envelope so parents can return the survey to you by a specific date. Give yourself enough time to be able to read them over before school begins.

Greeting Card Center

People love to receive cards and notes from children. Help children list birthdates and anniversaries of parents, siblings, and other adults that the students care about. Place this list where it is easily accessible to the students. Have in your greeting card center such supplies as brightly colored paper and construction paper, glue, glitter, markers, and other writing implements, scissors, and other supplies for decorations. When a family event occurs, allow the student time to design a card. This same center can be used for making cards for Jewish holidays, as well. The students can also make cards for nursing home residents or hospital patients.

Parental Involvement

The summertime, before the school year begins, is the best time to plan ways to get parents involved. Here are some practical suggestions.

Refrigerator Door Communication

The "Refrigerator Door" paper is one sheet of paper with a theme for the day, week, or month (depending on how often you want to send these papers home).

They can include one activity based on your unit of study, that families can do together, a riddle or puzzle, a recipe for an upcoming holiday; a short midrash on the weekly Torah portion, and also reminders of upcoming events that will be taking place in school.

Questions

Another source of communication would be a sheet titled "Questions Your Child Should Be Able to Answer." The questions would be based on the material covered in your unit of study. Sending question sheets home on a monthly basis will give the parents a good idea of what their children are learning in the classroom. It also gives the kids a chance to review and reteach the content.

Family Homework

How about some homework for the families? Plan a fun but simple educational project each month that students can work on with their families. Allow several weeks for them to complete the project. Here are a few ideas:

Form a travel agency and plan a dream vacation to Israel.
Create a book about Israel that includes a fact for each letter of the alphabet.
    (For a real challenge, use the Hebrew *alef-bet*.)
Make a book of family holiday recipes. Include one or two for each holiday.

Snack and Sharing

Encourage parents or even grandparents to provide a simple breakfast or snack in the classroom. This gives them a chance to catch up with what is taking place in school. Be aware of any food allergies.

Parental Talent

Prepare a sheet that has been divided into "tickets" that parents can cut apart and return to school. Include a cover letter describing the different skills that will be needed during the school year and when each will be needed. Some examples are driving for field trips; serving; baking; typing; helping with computers, music, or drama; videotaping; taking photographs; and speaking about a career. Parents fill in the tickets and return them for you to redeem as needed. Encourage parents to indicate any other talents they might have and wish to share.

Open Classroom

Parents really do want to know what is taking place in religious school. If possible, plan to have some regular meetings with all the parents of your class. These can be held as often as once a month, twice a semester, once each trimester, or with whatever frequency best suits.

Prepare a lesson plan! It is important that these meetings be well planned, so prepare as you would for a class with your students. You can have reading activities to give the parents an idea of what the students are covering in class, "make and take" projects, a game like Jeopardy or College Bowl, or brainstorming sessions to help parents support their child's Jewish education. You can also have a special program which the students have prepared. The idea is to make the meeting informative but entertaining at the same time so they will come back for the next one.

Letters to Parents

For an open house, provide theme-appropriate stationery and have each student write a letter to his or her parents telling them what the class has been doing in school. Place each letter in an envelope. The day of the open house, place each letter on the appropriate student's desk for the parents to enjoy. They can read their letter when they arrive or while they are waiting to talk to you. You may wish to provide stationery so parents can write their own letters in return. At the next class session, "deliver" these notes to students.

Some topic-specific ideas

- Ask each student to read with his or her parents a portion of the Bible or a text you are studying in the classroom. The students can interview their parents about their reaction to the reading.
- Ask students to poll their parents about an environmental issue and its relationship to Judaism.
- Have students explain their understanding of a Jewish historical event and ask their parents' opinion.
- Create a "Family Mission Statement" regarding the family's Jewish values. Ask each student to work with his or her family to create a family mission statement. What is the most important Jewish thing for that family to do? How can this goal be achieved?

End-of-the-Year Activities

How you end your year is as important as how you began it. Finishing on a strong note leaves students with positive feelings and sets the tone for next year.

CLASSROOM ACTIVITIES

End-of-Year Awards

Everyone likes to receive awards. Let the children decide what awards can be given. *Each student in the class should receive one!* Do some brainstorming and make a list of all the awards that could be given. Your list could look something like this:

Most congenial	Best attendance at worship service
Happiest	Best handwriting in Hebrew
Best attendance	Most helpful
Nicest Smile	Most Cooperative
Friendliest	Most Creative

Alternative

Several weeks before the end of the school year, ask each student to write his or her name at the top of a sheet of paper. Then pass their sheets around the "academy" (the class) and ask each student to write a *positive* statement about each student. To keep it confidential, the students are to fold the sheet down after writing on them. Collect the sheets, review the comments, and come up with an award for each student.

Of course, you will need to create an award certificate for each child that includes his or her name, award, and classmates' positive comments. Place this inside an envelope and write the child's name on the outside along with the name of the award. On the day of the presentation, let students take turns being the host. They will have fun saying, "May I have the envelope, please! This year's award goes to . . ."

A Keepsake for Students

Take a picture of each student. Give it to the child, along with a sheet of white drawing paper. Ask students to paste the picture near the top of the page and write their name above. Next, place these two statements on the board:

What is the best memory you have of the class from this past year?

What is the most important thing about Judaism you learned this year?

Ask the students to respond to these statements on the sheet of paper. When they have finished, gather up the papers. Photocopy and collate the pages so that each student has a booklet. Don't forget to add a cover page. (You can leave it blank for the students to decorate.) Pass the booklets out to the students on the last day of class. If students want, they can autograph the books for one another.

Another Keepsake

Send a booklet home so students can review some of their studies in a fun way. Create puzzles, games, pictures, dot-to-dots, mazes, and so on that cover some aspects of your different units of study from the past year. Copy a set for each student. Cover it with construction paper and staple together. Add a sticker on the cover with a title and the name of the student to whom the booklet belongs. Give these to the students on the last day of class to take home.

Knowledge Bowl

Ask each student to develop questions and answers on the different topics studied throughout the year. Give each student a different area to cover. Have the students write their question on one side of an index card and the answer on the other side.

To play Knowledge Bowl, divide the class into two teams. Place cards in a large bowl, then draw a card and ask a team the question. The teams take turns answering and earn 10 points for each correct answer. The team with the most points is the winner. If you want, invite the parents to join in the game on the last day. They will be pleased to see how much their children have learned throughout the year.

All the News That Is Fit to Print!

Let the students create a bulletin board, using the format of a newspaper's front page. Have the students collect various items related to the year's study, including photos, letters, articles, and so on. Students can arrange them below the "masthead" of the newspaper, then create headlines and captions about the different projects that took place during the year. You can invite parents to view the "late-breaking news cap" of the year.

A Flair for Learning

Give the students an opportunity to show off what they have learned during the year. To begin, brainstorm with the students a list of the different topics studied, achievements of the year, and favorite activities. Then have each student choose one topic from the list to do a project about. Students can use any form of media they desire, for example, posters, dioramas, or mobiles. They can complete the project in school or at home, depending on the amount of time you have allotted. On the last day of school, have the students display their projects throughout the room. Invite parents to view the "flair for learning" that took place during the year.

School T-shirts

Have each student bring a white T-shirt from home. You will also need: wide-tipped black permanent or fabric markers, different colors of fabric paint, and cardboard. To decorate the shirts, have students follow these steps:

1. Insert a piece of cardboard in the shirt to prevent paint or marker from bleeding through.
2. Write the school's name and year on the front of the T-shirt.
3. Have students dip their thumb in fabric paint, then make a thumbprint on the front of each classmate's shirt.
4. Instruct them to use a fine-tipped marker to sign their name below their thumbprint on each shirt.
5. Let the paint dry, then add fins and a tail to each thumb print with a fabric pen or indelible marker. Student can also add other decorations if they desire.
6. If there is time, after the shirts dry, students can decorate the back of the shirt with Jewish symbols representing the different topics of study covered during the year.

Mural of Year's Activities

The students can summarize their year of study with a giant mural. To begin, brainstorm with the students, making a list of all the different activities, special events, projects, and subjects covered each month.

Take a large piece of white butcher or art paper and place it on the floor. Divide the paper into the number of months in the school year. Break the class into small groups. Assign each group a month or two and ask children to draw pictures of what the class covered during that time. Upon completion, hang the mural in the classroom or the school hallway so everyone can admire their work.

Bibliography

This section contains books that could be helpful in your teaching. In addition to books referred to in the rest of *The Big Book of Terrific Teaching Ideas*, there are books included to provide the teacher with a stronger background in a subject. Many of these books have ideas or primary texts that can be used in the classroom to enhance lesson plans.

Bible and Other Jewish Texts

Bialik, Hayim N., and Ravnitzky, Yehoshua, eds. *The Book of Legends*. Translated by William G. Braude. New York: Schocken Books, 1995. This large volume contains collected legends and sayings from rabbinic tradition. Topics covered include commentary on the Bible, the stories of the Rabbis, and stories illustrating various Jewish values.

Fields, Harvey J. *A Torah Commentary for Our Times*. New York: UAHC Press, 1998. A Torah commentary that contains a brief summary, modern and classical commentary, and questions for each *parashah*.

Ginzberg, Louis. *The Legends of the Jews*. Baltimore: Johns Hopkins University Press, 1998. A multivolume anthology that compiles rabbinic stories commenting on the Bible.

Holtz, Barry, ed. *Back to the Sources*. New York: Touchstone Books, 1986. Contains short and easy-to-comprehend articles about the major genres of Jewish texts.

JPS Hebrew-English Tanakh. Philadelphia: Jewish Publication Society, 1999. The classic Hebrew-English volume.

Midrash Rabbah. London: Soncino Press, 1983. A ten-volume set that contains midrashic material on the five books of the Torah and the five *m'gillot.*

Plaut, W. Gunther, ed. *The Torah: A Modern Commentary.* New York: UAHC Press, 1981. The standard Torah text with English translation and extensive modern commentary and gleanings.

Soncino Hebrew/English Babylonian Talmud. 30 vols. London: Soncino Press, 1990.

Telushkin, Joseph. *Biblical Literacy.* New York: William Morrow, 2002. Contains short essays about major topics in the Bible.

Children's Books

Abraham, Michelle. *Shabbat Shalom!* New York: UAHC Press, 2003.

Ackerman, Karen. *Song and Dance Man.* New York: Knopf, 1988.

Baxter, Leon. *Let's Play Noah's Art.* Colorado Springs: Chariot Victor, 1995.

Cone, Molly. *Hello, Hello, Are You There God?* New York: UAHC Press, 1999.

Cone, Molly. *Who Knows Ten: Children's Tales of the Ten Commandments.* New York: UAHC Press, 1999.

Goldin, Barbara Diamond. *Night Lights: A Sukkot Story.* New York: UAHC Press, 2002.

Handelman, Maxine Segal. *The Shabbat Angels.* New York: UAHC Press, 2003.

Maisel, Grace, and Samantha Shubert. *A Year of Jewish Stories.* New York: UAHC Press, 2004.

Manushkin, Fran. *Come Let Us Be Joyful!* New York: UAHC Press, 2001.

Manushkin, Fran. *Sophie and the Shofar.* New York: UAHC Press, 2002.

Polacco, Patricia. *Mrs. Katz and Tush.* New York: Dell, 1994.

Rossoff, Donald. *The Perfect Prayer.* New York: UAHC Press, 2003.

Rothenberg, Joan. *Yettele's Feathers.* New York: Hyperion Press, 1996.

Schuman, Burt. *Chanukah on the Prairie.* New York: UAHC Press, 2003.

Education

Barish, Shirley. *The Big Book of Great Teaching Ideas.* New York: UAHC Press, 1998.

Joseph, Samuel. *The Madrikhim Handbook: A Training Program for Teenagers Working in Jewish Schools.* Los Angeles: Torah Aura, 1990.

Starin, Carol Oserin, and Wolfson, Ron. *Let Me Count the Ways: Practical Innovations for Jewish Teachers.* Los Angeles: Torah Aura, 1999.

Food

Biers-Ariel, Matt. *The Seven Species: Stories and Recipes Inspired by the Foods of the Bible.* New York: UAHC Press, 2003.

Levy, Faye. *1000 Jewish Recipes.* New York: John Wiley & Sons, 2000.

Nathan, Joan. *The Foods of Israel Today.* New York: Knopf, 2001.

_____. *Jewish Cooking in America.* New York: Knopf, 1996.

_____. *The Jewish Holiday Kitchen.* New York: Schocken, 1998.

Rauchwerger, Lisa. *The Chocolate Chip Challah and Other Twists on the Jewish Holiday Table.* New York: UAHC Press, 2000.

Roden, Claudia. *The Book of Jewish Food.* New York: Knopf, 1996.

General

Einstein, Stephen J., and Kukoff, Lydia, eds. *Introduction to Judaism*. New York: UAHC Press, 1999. An introduction to Judaism that provides an easily understandable description of major Jewish ideas and practices.

Roth, Cecil, ed. *Encyclopaedia Judaica*. Jerusalem: Keter, 1996. Eighteen-volume reference set that contains scholarly articles on every aspect of Judaism. Also available as a CD-ROM.

Syme, Daniel. *The Jewish Home*. Rev. ed. New York: UAHC Press, 2004. Contains explanations on major Jewish practices in the home including holidays and life-cycle events.

Telushkin, Joseph. *Jewish Literacy*. New York: William Morrow, 2001. Consists of brief essays on every aspect of Judaism.

Washofsky, Mark. *Jewish Living*. New York: UAHC Press, 2001. A guide to living a Jewish life in the contemporary world through modern Jewish practice.

God and Prayer

Hoffman, Lawrence. *The Way into Jewish Prayer*. Woodstock, VT: Jewish Lights, 2000. An easy-to-understand introduction to Jewish prayer and the means to make Jewish prayer meaningful.

Munk, Elie. *The World of Prayer*. New York: Philipp Feldheim, 1988. A look at Jewish prayer.

Sonsino, Rifat, and Syme, Daniel. *Finding God: Selected Responses*. New York: UAHC Press, 2002. An anthology of texts with commentary that discuss different ideas about God ranging from the Bible until modern times.

Wolpe, David. *Teaching Your Children about God*. New York: Perennial, 1995. An informed guide to teaching children about God.

Yedwab, Paul. *The God Book*. New York: UAHC Press, 2002. A book for young people that introduces them to different Jewish concepts of God. Includes "My God Diary" pages to help students formulate their own ideas.

History

Ben-Sasson, Haim H., ed. *A History of the Jewish People*. Cambridge, MA: Harvard University Press, 1985. An in-depth scholarly text that chronicles all of Jewish history.

De Lange, Nicholas. *The Illustrated History of the Jewish People*. New York: Harcourt, 1997.

Flohr, Paul Mendes, and Reinharz, Jehuda, eds. *The Jew in the Modern World*. New York: Oxford University Press, 1995. A compilation of primary texts from Jewish history in the modern age.

Leiman, Sondra. *The Atlas of Great Jewish Communities*. New York: UAHC Press, 2002. Meant for students, this colorful, dynamic history of Jewish communities around the world can be enjoyed by adults as well.

Marcus, Jacob Rader. *The Jew in the Medieval World*. Cincinnati: HUC Press, 1990. An anthology of primary texts from Jewish history in medieval times.

Holidays

Agnon, S. Y. *The Days of Awe*. New York: Schocken, 1965. A collection of texts from biblical accounts through modern interpretations related to the themes of the High Holy Days.

Cardin, Nina Beth. *The Tapestry of Jewish Time: A Spiritual Guide to Holidays and Life-Cycle Events*. West Orange, NJ: Behrman House, 2000. Inspiring connections to Jewish holidays and life-cycle events.

Elkins, Dov Peretz, ed. *A Shabbat Reader*. New York: UAHC Press, 1998. An anthology of different perspectives on the significance of Shabbat.

Goodman, Phillip, ed. *JPS Holiday Anthologies*. Philadelphia: Jewish Publication Society. This seven-volume series offers a wealth of material related to each particular holiday from Jewish writing, from the Bible to modern literature. Includes *The Hanukkah Anthology* (1976), *The Passover Anthology* (1961), *The Purim Anthology* (1949), *The Rosh Hashanah Anthology* (1970), *The Shavuot Anthology* (1975), *The Sukkot and Simchat Torah Anthology* (1973), *The Yom Kippur Anthology* (1971).

Heschel, Abraham Joshua. *The Sabbath*. New York: Noonday Press, 1951. A powerful discourse on the spiritual meaning of Shabbat.

Kaplan, Mordecai M. *The Meaning of God*. Detroit, MI: Wayne State University Press, 1995. Kaplan discusses his theology of God through his understanding of the significance of the holidays.

Knobel, Peter S., ed. *Gates of the Seasons: A Guide to the Jewish Year*. New York: CCAR, 1983. A survey of the holidays with detailed guidance on their observation.

Strassfeld, Michael. *The Jewish Holidays*. New York: Harper Collins, 1993. A comprehensive summary of the holidays with textual connections, historical context, and ideas for observance.

Israel

Sachar, Howard. *A History of Israel*. New York: Knopf, 1996. An in-depth history of Israel from the beginning of Zionism in the nineteenth century until the conclusion of the recent Oslo peace accords.

Tal, Eliyahu. *Whose Jerusalem?* Jerusalem, Israel: Gefen Books, 1997. An account of the different communities living in Jerusalem.

Tigay, Alan M., ed. *The Jewish Traveler*. Livingston, NJ: Jason Aronson, 1995. A collection of travel articles from *Hadassah Magazine*.

Jewish Values

Telushkin, Joseph. *The Book of Jewish Values*. New York: Bell Tower, 2000. A compilation of 365 topics on ethics, spirituality, and values.

Vorspan, Albert and Saperstein, David. *Jewish Dimensions of Social Justice*. New York: UAHC Press, 1998. Discussion on the Jewish commitment to social justice.

Life-Cycle

Diamant, Anita. *Choosing a Jewish Life: A Handbook for People Converting to Judaism*. New York: Schocken, 1998. A helpful book about the issues related to conversion.

_____. *The New Jewish Wedding*. New York: Fireside, 2001. An informative guide to creating a meaningful Jewish wedding.

_____. *Saying Kaddish: How to Comfort the Dying, Bury the Dead and Mourn as a Jew*. New York: Schocken, 1999. A useful and sensitive book dealing with a difficult subject.

Leneman, Helen, ed. *Bar Bat Mitzvah Basics: A Practical Guide to Coming of Age Together.* Woodstock, VT: Jewish Lights, 1996. Deals with preparation, the ceremony, the party, and the realities of today's families.

Salkin, Jeffrey. *Putting God on the Guest List: How to Reclaim the Spiritual Meaning of Your Child's Bar or Bat Mitzvah.* Woodstock, VT: Jewish Lights, 1996. How to make the journey more meaningful.

Quotations

Baron, Joseph, ed. *A Treasury of Jewish Quotations.* Livingston, NJ: Jason Aronson, 1997.

Gribetz, Jessica. *Wise Words: Jewish Thoughts and Stories through the Ages.* New York: William Morrow and Co., 1997.

Kolatch, Alfred, ed. *Great Jewish Quotations: By Jews and About Jews.* Middle Village, NY: Jonathan David, 1996.

Shea, Noah Ben. *Great Jewish Quotes: Five Thousand Years of Truth and Humor from the Bible to George Burns.* New York: Ballantine Books, 1993.

Judaism and the Environment

Bernstein, Ellen, ed. *Ecology and the Jewish Spirit.* Woodstock, VT: Jewish Lights, 1998. A series of essays about ecology within Judaism.

Biers-Ariel, Matt. *Solomon and the Trees.* New York: UAHC Press, 2002. Modern midrashic tale about King Solomon and his connection to nature.

Cone, Molly. *Listen to the Trees.* New York: UAHC Press, 1994. Collection of stories, readings, and texts on Judaism and the environment.